Bonds Now!

MAKING MONEY IN THE NEW FIXED INCOME LANDSCAPE

Marilyn Cohen and Chris Malburg

Publishers of the *Forbes Tax Advantaged Investor* newsletter

WILEY

John Wiley & Sons, Inc.

Published by John Wiley & Sons, Inc., Hoboken, New Jersey.
Published simultaneously in Canada.

For general information on our other products and services or for technical support, please contact our Customer Care Department within the United States at (800) 762–2974, outside the United States at (317) 572–3993 or fax (317) 572–4002.

Wiley also publishes its books in a variety of electronic formats. Some content that appears in print may not be available in electronic books. For more information about Wiley products, visit our web site at www.wiley.com.

Library of Congress Cataloging-in-Publication Data:

Cohen, Marilyn.
    Bonds now! : making money in the new fixed income landscape/ Marilyn Cohen and Chris Malburg.
        p. cm.
    Includes index.
    ISBN 978-0-470-54700-7 (cloth)
    1. Bonds. 2. Fixed-income securities. 3. Portfolio management. 4. Investments. I. Malburg, Christopher R. II. Title.
    HG4651.C6924 2010
    332.63′23–dc22   2009033771

Printed in the United States of America

10 9 8 7 6 5 4 3 2 1

We dedicate this book to Lt. Robert Andrew Cohen, Naval Intelligence Officer. You are the best of the best in life: Great nephew, caring person, and integrity personified. "Honor, courage, commitment" ... that's you. Ooh-rah, Rob.

Aunt Marilyn and Uncle Chris

Contents

Foreword

The credit crisis of 2008–2009 was brutal, not only for equities but also for bonds. The only safe harbor was Treasuries, yet for several months in 2009 even Treasury note and bondholders suffered losses as equities *and* junk bonds surged in value. This violence in the fixed-income securities markets underscores why investors badly need the sure, expert guidance of Marilyn Cohen. We know how crucial it is to have diversification in our portfolios, but how do we navigate the tricky markets of fixed-income securities—particularly Marilyn's specialty, bonds? Most issues don't have the liquidity one expects from stocks, and even mutual funds can experience uncomfortable spreads in some of their holdings. Yet bonds are crucial components—or should be—in the portfolios of millions of investors.

With *Bonds Now!* Marilyn Cohen has written a book giving us step-by-step ways to navigate the new, post–2008-credit-crisis bond market. Too often bond investors delegate control of their investments to their brokers. In these turbulent times it's understandable that you might want to hire a professional, but you should understand the strategies and tactics he or she will be using. Marilyn's book lays these out in an honest, forthright manner.

Too many individual bond investors make a buy and then never look at the position again—a big mistake as *Bonds Now!* shows. The credit crisis has changed the rules of engagement for bond investors; now they must learn how to navigate information sources, find a number of reliable news sources (such as *Forbes!*) and use several bond brokers to work their transactions.

To be a successful investor you need to understand the changes that have occurred in the bond market and be aware of new investment dos and don'ts. Those who ignore them will be condemned to follow in the footsteps of those whose bond portfolios suffered so much between 2008 and 2009. *Bonds Now!* gives a dead-on account of how the bond ratings game has changed, as well as how the usefulness of ratings and the assurance they once provided have flown out the window. Traditional bond ratings still provide some helpful information, but you have to know when and how to apply the ratings to your investment strategy.

Another crucial factor: corporate management teams. For bond investors this knowledge is critical. Management teams change: A company may have a history of being friendly to its bondholders but can suddenly change when a new CEO comes on board or economic circumstances fluctuate. Marilyn's book discusses reliable ways, regardless of the reason, to anticipate the effects of such changes. You can take specific steps in your bond portfolio to prevent damage from corporate executives who suddenly turn on their bondholders.

Marilyn has been the fixed-income securities columnist at *Forbes* for 14 years. I consider both *Bonds Now!* and the *Forbes Tax Advantaged Investor* newsletter essential reading for anyone who is serious about making money in the bond market. Both provide useful insights and specific recommendations (by CUSIP number) in the plain-speaking style that has become Marilyn's trademark.

Forbes is so convinced that bond investors need this information that we and Marilyn are offering a free three-month trial subscription to the *Forbes Tax Advantaged Investor* newsletter with the purchase of *Bonds Now!* They will give you two of today's most powerful tools for bond investors.

Take the time to study the *Bonds Now!* techniques, understand how they work, and then put them to use. To make this even easier, Marilyn has sprinkled critical Action Steps throughout her book, each containing specific instructions on how to implement the ideas in the preceding text. What could be clearer and easier?

Happy and profitable investing,
Steve Forbes

Preface

If you listen closely you can hear the Baby Boomers repeatedly chant, "No more equity risk, no more equity risk." They see the end zone of their careers. There's no time left to recoup losses incurred from foolish investment mistakes. The Baby Boom generation has suffered the tech wreck of 2000 and the credit crisis of 2008. The game clock to retirement is ticking. Many have lost a significant chunk of the nest egg they thought was set aside for their golden years. Most just ask for a foolproof way to protect what they have left.

The smart baby boomers—and there are millions of us—opened the welcoming door to bond investing. Timing is everything. Just as the door swung open, the bond market began transforming. Even now it continues to evolve. Before its morphing is finished, the bond market will be a more regulated and less liquid beast. There is a whole new set of rules on how to buy, what to buy, and when to buy in order to make money in the bond market. Ignore them and you are doomed to losses. Know them, use them, and you will not only protect your capital, but you will prosper.

Bonds Now! identifies the most recent changes in the bond market. It links the new rules of profiting in the bond market to new survival methods and fresh buy/sell principals. The book combines them all to show individual investors how to make smart bond investments in the post–credit crisis era.

We wrote this book for you, the individual bond investor. Perhaps you feel in the pit of your stomach that your broker deliberately fails to provide you the best and most current prices for your bond orders. Sound familiar? This little book shows how to deal with such lapses and many others in getting and judging bond intel.

Do you wonder if your investment portfolio can take you through retirement? You're in good company. There are 78 million Baby

Boomers in the same desperate boat. *Bonds Now!* shows you how to create a predictable income stream to subsidize your Social Security and retirement pension. Climb aboard. We sail on the tide, bound for bond investment safety and prosperity.

Bonds Now! shows you the new, post–credit crisis way of smart bond investing. It will improve your bond trading management skills. We'll teach you how to better manage your bond portfolio. Astute investors learn from past mistakes. *Bonds Now!* shows by example the costly errors of some investors, then, how to make the necessary corrections so they can never happen again. *Bonds Now!* is your fixed income GPS system. Use this book to chart a new, safer course through the changing bond landscape.

Bonds Now! picks up where the basic texts leave off. If you manage your own bond portfolio and you want to do it better, smarter, and achieve more profitable results, then this book is for you. Wall Street's consolidation of the banks, investment banks, and brokerage firms along with all the new regulations have changed the way investors conduct business. If you want your bond portfolio to profit from these new rules of engagement but don't know how, then you've come to the right place.

Each of the 14 chapters featured in *Bonds Now!* walks you through how the fixed income landscape has changed and what to do about it in your own investing. There is no technical *bond-speak* that only the bond geeks understand. In plain English, Chapter 1, Portfolio Survival, describes what changes the 2008 credit crisis caused and provides an overview of the techniques shown throughout the rest of the book.

The next chapters show how to use the new rules of engagement to build an impregnable fortress surrounding your bond portfolio; how to seize control from your broker when executing bond trades; and the silly mistakes others made so you won't repeat them.

With the technical aspects of bond trading under control, *Bonds Now!* moves on to the techniques that separate a successful bond investor from the others. We show: what a bond-friendly corporate management team looks like; how to identify an ego-maniac CEO; what the bond rating agencies did to precipitate the credit crisis; and how to use what little value they have left to offer. If bond analysis is something you delegate to your broker, Chapter 11 removes the mystery and cuts to the chase of what's important to know about a bond you think you want. From there the book focuses on the things only the bond experts use. They aren't talking. But we are. You'll see some of the mission-specific bonds with a particular purpose in your portfolio, what it means to have a sixth sense for trouble in a bond you own, and finally, we summarize the lessons learned.

Action Step

Throughout the book you'll see boxes labeled, **Action Step**. These are specific instructions—summarized and in plain English—that tell you just what to do. **Action Steps** convert the theory discussed in the chapter to practical use in your bond portfolio.

We know you'll enjoy reading *Bonds Now!* More important, we hope that you will use the ideas and concepts to boost the profitability of your bond investing.

About the Authors

As CEO of Los Angeles–based Envision Capital Management, Inc., **Marilyn Cohen** is one of the top bond managers in the country. Her 30-year financial career has included securities analysis at William O'Neil & Co., bond brokerage at Cantor Fitzgerald, Inc., and for the last 15 years founder and CEO of Envision Capital. She specializes in managing bond portfolios for individuals. For over 15 years Marilyn has written the bond column appearing in *Forbes* magazine. She is the author of *The Bond Bible* (Prentice Hall/New York Institute of Finance, 2000) and was technical editor for *Investing in Bonds for Dummies* (Wiley Publishing, Inc., 2007). Additionally, she is a popular guest on CNBC, Fox Business News, PBS, and the major broadcast networks, guiding individuals through the workings of the bond market in plain English.

As founder and Managing Editor of Writers Resource Group, Inc., **Chris Malburg** is an accomplished financial writer with over 4 million words in print spread among nine books (among them, *Business Plans to Manage Day-to-Day Operations,* John Wiley & Sons, Inc., 1993). Chris is a CPA, has an MBA, and is a former partner at investment banking powerhouse, Global Capital. Chris's clients and projects span securities broker/deals, automotive manufacturers, software companies, healthcare companies, and insurance and financial services enterprises.

Together, Marilyn and Chris publish the monthly *Forbes Tax Advantaged Investor* newsletter for bond investors.

CHAPTER 1

Portfolio Survival

Richard Lancaster ran a shaking hand through his silver hair. "What do you mean my 401(k) is worth only half of what it was last year?" he screeched at his Smith & Co. broker. "That was my retirement money."

Lancaster is an aerospace engineer living and working in Redondo Beach, CA. He is 60 years old and was hoping to retire in three years. At least he and wife, Ruth, own their home. And the kids have moved away and are self-sufficient.

"We needed every cent of that $2 million to generate income to live on," cried Lancaster. "Why didn't you tell me things were dicey? I would have sold out a year ago. Weren't you minding the store like you promised?"

That was Lancaster's first mistake: Putting his entire 401(k) account in the hands of a single stockbroker. What the broker hasn't told him yet is that he put half the portfolio in the corporate bond market. He figured it was safe enough for the old guy. It didn't generate much commission, but he fixed that on the front end by hugely marking up the bonds when he sold them into Lancaster's account from the firm's own inventory. Problem is, the value of those bonds has fallen just as much as the stocks. For some, he can't even get a bid from the broker who sold them in the first place.

It looks like Richard Lancaster will be working for the foreseeable future. His case isn't uncommon. If this hasn't happened to you, you probably know someone to whom it has. The good news is that you can do something about it so you don't become another casualty of the bond market.

1

Too many investors had their bond portfolios on cruise control throughout the 2008/2009 credit crisis. The result: Their portfolio values shrank by a third or more. We've heard way too many of these middle-aged and older investors shrug their shoulders, saying, "I'm in good company. Everyone has suffered a downturn in portfolio value. There was nothing anyone could do about it."

We call that stinkin' thinkin'. Certainly, few saw America's economic collapse coming. Wall Street and the rest of the professional investment community sure didn't. How could they? Such a collapse hadn't happened in their lifetime. That's half excusable. What isn't excusable is that so many individual investors are doing nothing about it. They think that if they stick to their old bond investment strategies and use the same hackneyed brokers they always have, somehow things will get better. They won't. The bond market targets such people and takes their money like a thief in the night.

Then there are the seasoned investors who understand that things have changed. Structurally changed. Some employ a new strategy when buying bonds for their retirement portfolios. Perhaps they got religion and now look at the underlying bond ratings rather than the rating of the unstable bond insurer. However, too few have applied this discipline to their *existing* bond portfolio. That's where the real risk lies. That's also where their emotional favorites reside. Many view these as untouchable. See the fallacy of their mistake? Read on.

Moody's Investor Services, one of the Big Three bond rating agencies, recently assigned its "negative outlook" to the creditworthiness of *all* the nation's local governments. This has never been done before. It should serve as fair warning to bond investors. Unless individual investors press the restart button on their investment strategies, their principal will continue eroding. Pretty soon they won't have enough money generating sufficient income on which to live. They will be forced to live on a lower economic level than they ever thought they would. Visualize a retirement without the ability to go to restaurants, take the trips you dreamed of, and buy gifts for the grandkids. Doesn't look very appealing, does it. All because many refused to change their investment habits, to employ a new strategy specifically designed to cope with and profit from the challenging economic environment in which we find ourselves. In other words, *to press the restart button for portfolio survival.*

No More Cruise Control

At one time in the not-too-distant-past—2008, in fact—fixed income investors could buy a municipal bond without much worry. They could put bonds in their securities portfolio and forget about them. Many counted their bond portfolio as their core nest egg—their safe money. They were on cruise control.

Bail out was something you did for fun from an airplane with a parachute. "Sure," they said, "municipalities have their problems. But they aren't in danger of imminent default on their bonds, are they?" Yes, some are. We'll show you how to spot them. Read on.

What Went Wrong in Bondland?

Lots. First came the problems with corporate bonds. During 2008, when the credit crisis reached critical mass, the spread between corporate bond yields versus those of Treasuries swelled to historic levels. This signaled the flight to quality as investors traded riskier corporates for more stable Treasuries. Investment-grade corporate bond prices began falling and didn't stop until they bottomed near the levels of junk bonds from just one year earlier. Then came a panic sell-off by the hedge funds. The hedgies had to meet insistent margin calls. They were selling stocks, bonds, real estate—anything not nailed down.

With these emergency margin calls came the first cries for bailout America. They came from those institutions that thought they were too large to fail. The TARP money given to banks was supposed to be their salvation. It wasn't. Instead it shackled management teams and prevented them from making the decisions needed to run their businesses without first asking the government's permission.

Government interventions—some call it the first steps toward nationalization—have changed the entire investment landscape. Individuals who ignore this change and who refuse to alter their investment strategies will pay the price.

 Action Step: Avoid Industries with Government Intervention

Never buy a corporate bond with even a hint of government participation, curiosity, or investment. Knowing what not to buy is often just as important as knowing what to buy. The Action Steps sprinkled throughout this book will tell you what to look for.

Municipal Bond Problems

Soon the corporate evils gravitated to the municipalities. We saw a symptom of the dilemma facing state and local bonds when five governors requested that the federal government provide $1 trillion in economic stimulus money—a mammoth bailout.

The five governors were John Corzine of New Jersey, David Patterson of New York, Deval Patrick of Massachusetts, Ted Strickland of Ohio, and James Doyle of Wisconsin. Take special note if you own bonds issued by these states. In fact, these funds were supposed to fill in their own state's budget gaps but couldn't easily get the job done.

As if that trillion-dollar number wasn't scary enough, these governors wouldn't come to terms with the spending cuts needed to ensure we taxpayers don't have to bail them out a second or third time. Excessive leverage caused the 2008 financial implosion. That, and enterprises thought too big to fail were living beyond their means, then crying for a bailout when their capital dwindled to perilous levels and they couldn't pay their bills. That now infamous word, bailout, has recently entered our every day lexicon. It forces us to accept the results of what we've allowed to happen.

We don't have to drill down much deeper to connect these events to municipal bonds. Our states and cities cannot borrow their way out of these self-created deficits. Further adding to bondholder's travails is that five of the twelve largest municipal bond underwriters and trading desks have merged or exited the business entirely. This means that now there are fewer execution resources available to bond investors. And there is less capital being allocated to municipal bond inventories.

Essential Liquidity

Without an adequate number of institutions to execute bond trades, liquidity is sucked right out of the market. Without liquidity, investors are at the mercy of only a few bond dealers who can name whatever price they wish. Watch for the concept of liquidity. We'll pound on it throughout this book.

Liquidity in Bondland means having sufficient buyers and sellers for a particular issue to maintain an orderly, arms-length market that is driven by price, yield, spread, and supply and demand rather than a single participant with the ability to control the market.

Liquidity has several components. First is the number of underwriters, issuers, and dealers. Investors must be able to play one bond source off the others. If the price of one broker/dealer is off the market, his competition will likely offer it at a better price. Another source of liquidity is the size of the issue. Bond investors—the savvy ones, at least—only buy corporate bond issues with a minimum size of $250 million. Such size prevents a single investor from capturing the majority of the issue. If you hold a few bonds in a thinly traded issue, you'll rarely get a fair price. That is, if you can scare up any bids at all.

You may ask, "What about my bond fund? Risk is spread over a whole trainload of different bonds. Surely such diversity provides safety." Untrue. In the credit crisis, municipal and corporate bond funds had massive outflows. Funds without sufficient cash to honor investor demands for their money were forced to sell assets (bonds held in their portfolios). The Street smelled blood in the water. The funds were forced to take what they could get for their assets. Fund prices plunged. Panic set in. Investors tripped over one another, seeking the safety and security of Treasuries. This drove T-bills to a negative rate of return.

Bond Downgrades

We've dedicated Chapter 7 to the rating agencies. Watch for them to downgrade more bonds. This is due to the municipal bond issuers'—the states, cities, and school districts—overreliance on property tax revenues amid the bear market in housing. Property taxes account for 72 percent of local government income throughout the nation. The steep decline in property values caused these same governmental entities to suffer a huge revenue shortfall. As revenues fall, so does the likelihood that the issuer can maintain its debt service on the bonds it issued. The less coverage of debt obligations a bond issuer has, the lower its bond rating. The cities and counties spent money as if property values would never decline. They suffered dearly when housing values plummeted like that blue ice that sometimes falls off of airliners and comes crashing to earth.

As the inevitable happened and property tax revenue began shrinking, many municipalities could not stop the spending. They dug an even bigger hole by issuing revenue and tax anticipation notes to bridge the cash flow gap that their dwindling reserves should have covered.

These tax anticipation notes are supposed to be a temporary, short-term way of managing cash flow. As property tax revenues rise again and are collected, part of the money is used to repay the tax anticipation notes. The problem is, not only are property tax revenues not rising, but also the rest of the massive budget deficit is laying claim to the same money—that is, when it's finally collected. Suddenly, muni bondholders see their formerly safe investments as being subject to unprecedented risk. Who knew? We did. Now you do, too. No more excuses. No more tears. Let's get busy fixing the problem.

Also in Chapter 7, The Bond Rating Agencies, we will cover the massive amount of corporate bond defaults and downgrades post credit crisis. Fallen Angels, that's the sweet, peaceful phrase that Wall Street calls investment grade bonds that fall into the junk bond category. Historically, when an investment-grade corporate bond becomes junk, it's a very long, arduous climb back up to the promised land of investment grade.

Pushing the Restart Button

This book is all about new bond market survival rules and strategies. The landscape has changed. So must your bond investment strategy. Use the new market rules found here to your advantage and not only will you survive, but you'll thrive.

The New Bond Strategies

Even the savviest investors have had to change. The rules are being rewritten even as regulatory guidelines remain in flux. You may have invested the same way for decades. Now you must change. You may look at your decimated portfolio and say, "It's only an aberration—a long and deep one—but still just an aberration. Things will get back to normal any day now." It's not an aberration, and many things will never be the same again. The strategies of fixed income investing have changed forever.

Bond Insurance—Fageddaboudit

Buy only good quality municipal and corporate bonds that can weather the economic downturn on their own without depending on bond insurance. Buy bonds whose own ratings justify your confidence and investment dollars.

There are bond ratings, and then there are bond ratings. Be sure you know what you're looking at. The Big Three bond rating agencies (Moody's, Standard and Poor's, and Fitch) now assign two ratings to many municipal bonds. One has to do with the default insurance a particular issue may have. The other is the credit quality on the municipal bonds as a stand-alone—the underlying rating. If a bond is insured by a stable insurer such as Berkshire Hathaway Assurance that carries a Moody's rating of Aa1 and a Standard & Poor's rating of AAA, then chances are the underlying credit quality of the municipal bond is a minimum of A rated. The municipal bond insurers, both past and present, insured for a zero default rate. That was before so many municipalities hit the wall and suffered cash shortfalls.

However, if a bond is insured by a suspect firm such as National-Re (formerly MBIA Insurance Corp.), to which Moody's assigned Baa1 and Standard & Poor's assigned AA– ratings, then there's more to the story. Most of the bond insurers have problems. Many have had their ratings withdrawn entirely or have been placed on the rating agency's negative watch lists.

Note that the credit crisis and bear market in stocks have even taken their toll on the mighty Berkshire Hathaway. Stripped of its AAA rating, Moody's has dropped Berkshire's ratings to Aa1. Still a superior rating, but one notch lower than it was. Moody's cited the decline in equities, derivatives, and the economic downturn as the primary reasons for the downgrade. Even the vaunted Berkshire

Hathaway now has a chink in its armor. Understand that all ratings change over time. By the time you read this, they will have changed again.

There's real concern about bond issuer defaults. The insurance companies do not have sufficient reserves to make good on all those shaky bond deals they insured. When the avalanche of defaults occurs, they may be unable to pay everyone they owe. In other words, their insurance isn't worth much. So goes the bond's rating, which directly reflects the insurance company's rating.

It only took the bond insurers a few years to destroy their business. They accomplished this by insuring collateralized debt obligations (CDOs) and shaky mortgage-backed securities.

Underlying Credit Rating: The Real Test

The rating agencies are historically slow to change their ratings for fear of stepping on the toes of those who pay them. The result is that you must look at the *underlying* rating, that is, a rating that considers just the creditworthiness of the issuer *without regard* to the insurance.

Corporate bond defaults are not that uncommon. According to *Forbes* newsletters, over 200 corporate bond issues totaling some $20 to $50 billion default in a typical year. In addition, there are 300 to 400 corporate bond defaults and bankruptcies that remain unsettled. Expect that number to increase over the next few years. Recession reduces the value of corporate assets. Those remaining banks that can lend money will refuse to do so for fear of further compromising their already damaged balance sheets. The government's TARP money helps only a little, since some of the banks are doing absolutely everything they can to repay money that many didn't want or need in the first place.

 Action Step: Match Your Bonds with Your Risk Tolerance

Invest in a bond only if the *underlying rating* meets your risk criteria. Likewise for the bonds already in your portfolio. Don't keep any bonds whose underlying rating fails to meet your tolerance for risk. Sell and replace them with more stable bonds. See Chapter 7, The Bond Rating Agencies, for a table showing the meaning of the bond rating system.

The Safest Municipal Bond Categories

There are just seven bond categories we consider absolutely safe. Our criteria for safety revolve around two things: The bond's repayment source and who pays the bondholders in the event the issuer cannot. Here are the seven safest municipal bond categories.

Prerefunded Bonds

Bonds that were issued some time ago carried higher coupons than the current market. That's why municipalities issue new bonds at lower coupon rates to replace the old bonds. It's a simple refinancing. The municipality invests the proceeds to cover the principal and interest. Essentially, the bonds are refunded (or refinanced) in advance of either the next call date or the maturity—prerefunded or preres in bond vernacular. Investors who buy these prerefunded bonds are guaranteed prompt payment of their interest and principal because the funds are escrowed with an independent institution until they mature and are repaid.

There is a risk—but only to those investors who are unwary or unobservant. The collateral used in the escrow account must be money good. Before you buy a prerefunded bond or one that is escrowed until maturity, make sure the collateral is a SLGS (State and Local Government Series security, pronounced *Slug*). These are special Treasuries with yields that are custom-cut to match those of the old bond issue being replaced. SLGS are used exclusively in escrow accounts. They cannot be traded and are therefore sold directly to the escrow accounts by the U.S. Treasury.

Do not accept a prerefunded bond whose escrow collateral is a Fannie Mae or Freddie Mac security. The federal government has not given its explicit guarantee to Freddie Mac or Fannie Mae—they've only given an *effective* guarantee. That's not good enough. Figures 1.1 and 1.2 show what the Freddie and Fannie collateral looks like on a Bloomberg page.

General Obligation Bonds (GOs)

Most bond professionals consider General Obligation bonds among the safest of the fixed income instruments. GOs have the ability to tap additional tax revenues in the event of an economic shortfall. Since the taxing agencies have the (theoretical) authority for unlimited taxation to pay their bills, the GOs should be money good regardless

```
57582NXS9 Muni DES                                                  Muni  DES
Enter 66 <GO> to Msg DES.
            MUNICIPAL  BOND  DESCRIPTION Page  1/  5
MASSACHUSETTS ST                                          CUSIP:57582NXS(9)
PREREFUNDED-CONS LN-C-MBIA-IBC
TICKER: MAS    CPN: 5¼    MATURITY:11/01/2030 DATED: 7/01/2002 STATE:MA
7) THE SINKING FUND PAYMENTS DUE ON 2029 AND 2030 HAVE BEEN REFUNDED AND WILL BE
9) TDH MSRB Trades                     |            TRADING INFORMATION
10) SCN Issuer's Material Events       |1ST SETTLE DATE                 7/02/2002
       SECURITY INFORMATION            |NEXT SETTLEMENT DATE            7/23/2009
ISSUE TYPE     GENERAL OBLIGATION LTD  |INTEREST ACCRUAL DATE           7/01/2002
MATURITY TYPE  1) CALL, 3) SINK        |1ST COUPON DATE                11/01/2002
COUPON TYPE    FIXED, OID              |27) RFNG  REFUNDED INFORMATION
PRICE/YIELD @ ISSUE  99.699/  5.270    |PREREFUNDED 11/01/12 @ 100
COUPON FREQ.   SEMI-ANNUAL             |COLLAT:FHLMC( 77%)
TAX PROVISION  FED & ST TAX-EXEMPT     |      FNMA( 12%)
FORM           REGISTERED              |      FHL BANKS(  7%)
               RATINGS      WATCH OUTLK|      US TREASURY OBLIG(  4%)
MOODY'S        WR                      |ORIGINAL CUSIP: 57582NEU
S&P            AA
 UNDERLYING    AA
12) RCHG Rating changes
33) Setup rating alerts

Hit page for additional des, call sch, sinking fund sch, os notes information.
Australia 61 2 9777 8600 Brazil 5511 3048 4500 Europe 44 20 7330 7500 Germany 49 69 9204 1210 Hong Kong 852 2977 6000
Japan 81 3 3201 8900      Singapore 65 6212 1000      U.S. 1 212 318 2000      Copyright 2009 Bloomberg Finance L.P.
                                                                             G407-87-1 20-Jul-09 17:40:09
```

Figure 1.1 Avoid Fannie & Freddie Used as Collateral—Agency Prere

Source: Bloomberg Finance L.P.

```
86481RAM9 Muni DES                                                  Muni  DES
Enter 66 <GO> to Msg DES.
            MUNICIPAL  BOND  DESCRIPTION Page  1/  4
SUFFOLK VA INDL DEV AUTH      ECONOMIC DEV REV            CUSIP:86481RAM(9)
HOTEL & CONFERENCE CTR PROJ
TICKER: SUFDEV CPN: 5⅛      MATURITY:10/01/2035 DATED: 9/15/2003 STATE:VA
9) TDH MSRB Trades                     |            TRADING INFORMATION
       SECURITY INFORMATION            |1ST SETTLE DATE                10/08/2003
ISSUE TYPE     REVENUE BONDS           |NEXT SETTLEMENT DATE            7/23/2009
MATURITY TYPE  1) CALL, 3) SINK        |INTEREST ACCRUAL DATE           9/15/2003
COUPON TYPE    FIXED, OID              |1ST COUPON DATE                 4/01/2004
PRICE/YIELD @ ISSUE  97.920/  5.260    |WEEK OF SALE                    9/29/2003
COUPON FREQ.   SEMI-ANNUAL             |27) RFNG  REFUNDED INFORMATION
TAX PROVISION  FED & ST TAX-EXEMPT     |PREREFUNDED 10/01/13 @ 100
FORM           BOOK-ENTRY              |COLLAT:ST&LOC GOVT SERIES(100%)
               RATINGS      WATCH OUTLK|NOTES:   Personal  Office   Firm
S&P           NOT RATED                |          24) NOT  25) ONTS  26) FNTS
FITCH         NOT RATED                |11) CF View Documents
12) RCHG Rating changes                |29) Issuer Web Page
33) Setup rating alerts
            CREDIT SUPPORT
CREDIT SUPPORT:ACA

Hit page for additional des, call sch, sinking fund sch information.
Australia 61 2 9777 8600 Brazil 5511 3048 4500 Europe 44 20 7330 7500 Germany 49 69 9204 1210 Hong Kong 852 2977 6000
Japan 81 3 3201 8900      Singapore 65 6212 1000      U.S. 1 212 318 2000      Copyright 2009 Bloomberg Finance L.P.
                                                                             G407-87-1 20-Jul-09 17:40:53
```

Figure 1.2 Instead Accept SLGS as Prerefunded Collateral

Source: Bloomberg Finance L.P.

of the economy. Further, GOs usually stand in front of most other bonds. Except, of course, in California. There, the school bonds have first claim on tax revenues, followed by the GOs. Your state may have a constitutional amendment like California's regarding priority of payments. Find out where you stand in the repayment line.

Revenue Bonds with a Secondary Repayment Source

The industry fondly calls such revenue bonds *double-barreled tax exempts*. These munis are a hybrid general obligation bond. However, they're safer than ordinary GOs because the sources of repayment are guaranteed by two separate and distinct revenue streams. Only the *full faith and creditworthiness* of the issuing state or municipality backs regular general obligation bonds. Double-barreled bonds have this same guarantee along with an alternative source of repayment revenue. In the event that one of the revenue streams is compromised (such as the revenue shortfall from sales tax declines), investors still have the security provided by the alternative source of funds. A double-barreled sewer revenue bond is a good example. Such a bond is primarily funded by revenue from the sewer it built, and it is backstopped by the local tax revenues if there's a problem.

Because of the dual source of repayment, double-barreled bonds are safer than regular general obligation bonds. With municipalities struggling and default rates rising, a double repayment source is a big plus.

Double-barreled bonds are hard to find. When you do find them, they may be priced a little higher than other general obligation bonds. You may have to pay for the added safety.

One of the largest double-barreled issuers is the California Economic Recovery. These bonds are backed by a special one-quarter cent pledge to California's sales tax revenues. Then, if needed, they are further backed by the full faith and credit of California. Even though California's economic problems (a $26 billion budget deficit as of this writing) probably won't go away anytime soon, an alternative source of payment reassures investors and makes the bonds more marketable.

Essential Service Revenue Bonds

These are revenue bonds issued for really important infrastructure projects such as the sewers and water facilities. Because revenue from property owners who use these facilities repays these bonds, they're generally considered low risk. However, be sure that the issuer is a stable, mature area where property taxes are consistent. Do not buy water and sewer bonds from an issuer that is new and depends on attracting new residents to a new housing development. Further, stay away from issuers whose tax base is eroding because people are being foreclosed with no new owners in sight.

First Mortgage Bonds

First Mortgage bonds are issued by corporations. They give investors the first lien on specific property owned by the issuing corporation. In the event of default, First Mortgage bondholders have the right to seize company property and equipment in order to secure repayment. Seizing and selling property on behalf of bondholders rarely is necessary (and would always be handled by the bond's trustees). More often, the company reorganizes and arranges payment for the bondholders, since the lien gives it no choice but to satisfy the claims.

First Mortgage bonds provide investors an extra safeguard if bankruptcy occurs. In a rising default environment, they're a good safety net. They also earn a decent yield.

However, there's some downside. Because the debt is more secure, the yield isn't always as high as unsecured debt. Remember, there's a rate for every risk. Even so, the yields are still attractive for such a low risk investment, and are certainly higher than alternatives like Treasuries.

Senior Secured Bonds

As with mortgage bonds, the pledge of specific assets as collateral, back senior secured bonds. This means that in the event of default and bankruptcy, bondholders can seize the collateral assets. The best secured bonds employ assets held in a third party trust as their collateral. This could be real estate mortgages as seen above or equipment trust certificates.

The problem with secured bonds is maintaining the assets in a salable condition while bondholders await their liquidation and disposition of the proceeds. Usually bondholders lack the expertise and ability to either maintain or sell the underlying assets.

Senior secured bonds with underlying assets as collateral increase the safety but in practice don't really do much for aggrieved investors.

We still hope that the issuer does not default on its interest and principal payments. Time is much better spent analyzing the issuer's ability to service its bond debt rather than the value of the secured assets offered as collateral.

Unsecured Bonds

Not far behind the safety curve are unsecured bonds. These depend on the issuer's ability to pay interest and principal. They are backed by nothing more than faith in the issuer's promise to pay. Should the issuer become bankrupt, seniority is an issue. First, the banks get paid. Next come the senior bonds—secured, then unsecured—which get first dibs on whatever is left, after attorney's fees, of course.

 Action Step: Steer Clear of Sub-Debt

Don't buy bank-subordinated debt (such as Citigroup subordinated bonds). The government demanded conversion of all preferred shares into common stock. This had the effect of moving the preferred stock holders from near the top of the payment ladder to the very bottom. In no way were the preferred shares ever contractually convertible into common stock. The bond market reaction to such an unprecedented governmental action in a non-Communist country was swift and painful: Citigroup subordinated debt and all bank subordinated debt traded at significantly wider spreads to Treasuries and senior debt than ever before. Bond prices dropped like a rock. Investors worried that if the government can do that to preferred shareholders, subordinated debt may be next.

Warning: Avoid Interest Rate Swaps

Municipalities use interest rate swaps in an attempt to lower municipal bond interest costs. The most frequently used swaps locked in fixed borrowing costs on variable rate debt. As the floor fell out of the interest rate market, local municipalities were horrified to find their bond interest payments tripled or quadrupled due to these toxic swaps. Many small municipalities received cash up front for these deals. They thought it was manna from heaven and spent the money. In fact, it was a deal with the devil.

You need look no further for the reason Jefferson County, Alabama, the schools in Philadelphia, the City of Detroit, and local California governments to see the disaster created by interest rate swaps. Each is all but bankrupt as a result of the interest rate swap contracts it did.

Why should you care? Because lurking in your portfolio may be a municipal bond with one or several interest rate swap contracts attached. If rates go against these issuing municipalities, their ability to service the debt—debt that you own—will be in serious jeopardy. Call your broker and demand an analysis of each muni in your account. Have him study the most recent Moody's or Standard & Poor's reports. There's almost always a discussion section about interest rate swaps if any exist with that bond. If your broker complains about the work involved, get a new broker. This is important to your financial survival.

These are just the first few new rules of engagement for bond investing. Know them. Follow them. Chapter 2 shows you how to employ them to your advantage.

2

New Rules of Engagement

Don't whine about how things have changed in Bondland. Facts are facts. This economic and credit crisis created a sea change in the way all investors manage their portfolios. The smart ones will see these changes and take them for the new reality they represent. Those who refuse to recognize that something historic occurred are destined to continue whittling down their investments until there is nothing left.

Our mission here is to identify for you exactly what has changed in Bondland. We'll provide insight as to the way things used to work. Perhaps this is the way you are still investing. Then we'll shine a light on the risk you take by continuing to conduct business as usual. Finally, we'll show you the new rules of engagement of which every investor should be aware. Let's roll.

The Way Things Were

It used to be that you could buy municipal bonds and investment grade corporates without worry as to price, viability of the issuer's business, or whether they would default. Not any more. Here are some of the rules of engagement investors once assumed would hold true no matter what.

Government Agency Debt Is as Good as Gold

This assumption no longer holds water. Just look what the U.S. government did to Fannie Mae and Freddie Mac preferred stock holders. Such agencies of the U.S. government were once considered among the safest investments around. Preferred stock was high up on the capital food chain should something go wrong. In other words, preferred stock holders would be paid long before common stock holders. The U.S. government crashed the party by putting both companies into a conservatorship. Overnight they forbade Fannie Mae and Freddie Mac from paying any more preferred stock dividends. Now, understand that preferred stock doesn't usually appreciate in value. The only reason to hold it is for the preferred dividends, which always paid like clockwork. Many regional banks held these agencies' preferred stock. It was safe, gave a nice return and it counted toward their Tier 1 capital requirements. Suddenly, with no more preferred dividends, the value of this stock immediately went to almost nothing. The pension funds as well as individual investors who thought they held something that was truly bulletproof woke up one morning to find their preferred stock portfolios decimated. Billions of investors' stock value was lost, never to be recovered. The regional banks had another problem—suddenly many were undercapitalized according to federal regulations. This single decision by the U.S. government sent the banking system reeling.

It's Okay to Take Risk on Good Companies

America's capitalistic system used to reward those who studied companies and did their homework. Smart investors combed through the balance sheets, identifying assets, toting up cash, and their equivalents. They'd run the financial ratios to see how much leverage the company had and what the interest coverage was. Sometimes they uncovered a well-capitalized company with a conservative approach to its business and its finances. They called these *good companies*. They took what they thought was an appropriate risk and bought these so-called *good companies'* bonds. To their horror, they discovered management of these good companies with the most conservative balance sheets had little idea what their assets were composed of. Neither, apparently, did their public accounting firms that conducted the audits and attested to the fairness of the financial statement presentations.

The financial services industry is an example. The banks thought they had properly reserved for all contingencies associated with the collateralized debt obligations backed by subprime mortgage loans. With such naive assurance, they issued and bought derivative securities by the boatload—also linked to the subprime market. Wall Street was pressuring management to juice up earnings. These were the high-yielding products that would get them there.

Supposedly seasoned executives who were paid tens of millions a year for their wisdom forgot the first rule of investing: There's a rate for every risk. Remember that; you'll see it again. There's a rate for every risk. What they found was a cesspool of toxic loans on which their bonds floated like oil scum. They were forced to write down the value of these investments. Bank stocks plummeted and with it, so did the value of their bonds. This cost the bondholders billions of dollars in lost value for what they thought was a moderate risk on a good company.

CEOs Rewarded; Investors Punished

It used to be that market forces punished companies and their heads who failed to execute their promised business plans and that ran their businesses into the ground. Witness the securities firm, Bear Stearns. Two of their hedge funds incurred horrendous losses. With its cash reserves severely depleted, there was ultimately a run on the bank. On March 16, 2008, the Federal Reserve and U.S. Treasury cobbled together a deal for JPMorgan Chase to buy Bear Stearns for just 7 percent of its market value.

The stock of bond insurer, Ambac, lost more than 90 percent of its market value during 2008. Ambac incurred massive losses due to its ill-advised forays into structured finance—derivative securities backed by subprime mortgages. Ambac's investors were devastated. Yet, four of the Company's top executives received a combined total of $3 million in performance bonuses. CFO Sean Leonard received a $950,000 cash bonus. Executive Vice President Douglas Renfield-Miller got $550,000. Chairman Michael Callen received $975,000, and Chief Executive Officer David Wallis garnered $500,000. Who says you can't prosper by failing?

If You Can't Trust the Auditor's Opinion . . .

Once upon a time a company's financial statements had some credibility. Especially if they were audited by one of the Final Four CPA firms. This naiveté has become just another fairy tale. Today, the public accounting profession has tarnished its credibility by failing to understand the business risks its clients undertake. Shortcuts and corner-cutting by unseasoned staff has become a way of life to complete complex audits on time and on budget. As for profits, they too have become a matter of opinion.

The result is supposedly solid balance sheets that are actually stuffed with credit default swaps and interest rate swaps. These toxic instruments have levels of liability that are largely unknown. The accountants haven't been able to come up with an accurate estimate of potential loss. Nor have they been successful in requiring their clients to reserve against that loss. Doing so would bring down earnings, causing the stock price to plummet and a likely loss of that client. So whom can you trust? Just yourself and your own good judgment.

Three Fixed Income Categories of Safety

Where can you hide your money during a credit crisis? You used to be safe in putting your retirement accounts or personal money into Treasuries, government agencies, or municipal bonds. We saw above how quickly with one wave of the government intervention wand agencies such as Fannie Mae and Freddie Mac can wipe out a lifetime of savings. Certain municipal bonds aren't much better unless you know what you're doing. That leaves just Treasuries. As of this writing, the return on Treasuries is miniscule, but they're still safe.

Unintended Consequences

None of these former rules of engagement work in the middle of the worst credit meltdown since the Great Depression. Since September 2008 the U.S. government has placed Fannie Mae and Freddie Mac under government conservatorship. The U.S. government became the majority shareholder of insurance giant, AIG. Indeed, writer Carol Loomis described the U.S. government's relationship with AIG in a magazine piece he wrote as a comparison with the 1942 movie *The Man Who Came to Dinner*. In that movie the unbearable Sheridan Whiteside comes to dinner, falls, and injures his hip on the front steps. He stays and stays, driving the hosts insane. AIG has come to the U.S. government's table—the taxpayer's, really—and refuses to leave. What started as an $85 billion loan has ballooned to $175 billion with no end in sight.

The U.S. Treasury chose to allow one broker/dealer (Bear Stearns) to survive with a new owner, JP Morgan Chase. But the same government decision makers refused to extend a similar rescue package to Lehman Bros. Instead they left it to swing in the breeze until it collapsed. These decisions and others by the government set in motion a series of unintended consequences in the credit markets.

By forcing the major U.S. money center banks to accept TARP money (Troubled Asset Relief Program), the U.S. government has created a *de facto* nationalization of the U.S.' banking system. The U.S. taxpayers were suddenly the borrower, lender, and spender of last resort. This *de facto* nationalization started the landslide that led to such radical changes in the rules of engagement for bond investors.

Rules for profitable bond investing have come and gone over the decades. Investors may not like it, but that's the real world. Now, more than ever, it's important that we know what the new rules are and how to apply them. The problem comes when no one—not even the governmental overseers—know what the new rules of engagement are. Indeed, the U.S. government is writing the rules as it goes along. Repayment of TARP monies is one example. Many banks didn't want this money and the onerous restrictions that went along with it. They repaid their TARP accounts to get out of this deal with the government devil just as fast as they could.

Corporate officer compensation and employee bonuses are rules that appear in flux. No one really knows where the ball will stop bouncing. All these are fluid situations that create confusion and uncertainty in the credit markets. Where there's uncertainty, there exists instability. This instability requires investors to change their approach to fixed income investing. That's the origin of the new rules of engagement.

New Rules of Engagement

Learning from past mistakes and observing the consequences of governmental interaction with free markets has brought about a series of new rules of engagement. Follow them and you'll have a fighting chance at not only preserving your wealth but in taking advantage of a fluid situation and actually prospering because of it. Ignore the new rules of engagement and your investment portfolio will sink like the Titanic. Here are the new rules of engagement.

Keep Fixed Investments Simple and Understandable

You probably knew that. But did you follow your own advice? If you didn't, you're in good company. Most people who knew this new rule of engagement didn't follow it. They reasoned not with their head but with the greed-gene we all possess. The point is, if you can't easily understand the deal, then walk away no matter what the yield. When faced with a sure-fire, can't-miss deal with returns double the market, walking away may sound stupid. Almost like you're leaving money on the table. And for a time it might appear that you did.

That is the story clients of money manager turned Ponzi schemer, Bernie Madoff, tell. Madoff reported huge returns every year to his clients. They smiled with satisfaction at his firm's internally prepared statements of their account's growing value. How could they yank out their money when Bernie was reporting a 12 percent return while everyone else was getting 5 percent or less? Madoff's explanation was so complicated and obfuscated that clients couldn't understand it. So they shut up and went along for fear of rocking the boat and being asked to leave Bernie's care and oversight. Imagine how these clients—both the sophisticated, and the unschooled—felt seeing their personal money manager whom they entrusted with their life savings being perp-walked before the TV cameras, hands cuffed behind his back

The truth is, that those who followed the rule of entering only simple and understandable investments came out one hell of a lot better than those who bought financial instruments whose structure was incomprehensible to even the most experienced professionals. The list of indecipherable products to avoid includes these three categories of fixed income instruments:

Structured Securities   The structure refers to the coupon's linkage with an outside index. Many such securities compute coupons as a percentage of the greater of the 5-, 10-, or 30-year constant maturing Treasury. Almost always such structured securities have derivatives behind them. Let this be a big, fat warning sign to stay away. The reason is that the income stream is not fixed and is uncertain. It is driven by something totally unrelated. Yet guaranteeing a fixed income is why investors own fixed income securities in the first place. Stick to this discipline.

LIBOR Range Notes   The coupons are tied to a range of interest rates in London Interbank Offered Rate (LIBOR) at a specific time or over a period of time. The language defining the coupon computations often reads as if its author was an insane lawyer determined to confuse investors and conceal the truth about these securities. It succeeded.

SmartNotes, DirectNotes, and Internotes Most investors who owned them failed to ask how easy it would be to sell these securities should they ever want to. This omission is understandable. After all, these notes were issued by such sterling and steadfast companies as GMAC (SmartNotes), the financing arm of General Motors, InCapital (Internotes), and Merrill Lynch (DirectNotes). Who would ever think entire industries would hit the skids and that making the interest and principal payments would become a problem for such companies? Yet only a little common sense in looking at the issue size of such notes would have told them that such small ($14–25 million) deals had no liquidity whatsoever and would likely be impossible to sell.

They were. Prices for the GMAC SmartNotes fell further than the large liquid GMAC global bonds. The reason? You guessed it—lack of liquidity. The brokers that sold the bonds had no interest in buying them back.

Determine Your Broker's Fixed Income Expertise

Most investors have been using their broker for years. They've established a relationship with him. They trust him. The thinking among so many investors is, "So my broker lost a third of my net worth. So did everyone else's broker. It's not his fault."

Yes, it is. The safety and welfare of your investment portfolio is first your responsibility, then your broker's or money manager's. Some of the money lost in the bond market was caused by incompetent advice proffered by "professionals" who didn't know what they were doing. Many of these were relatively savvy stock jockeys. But when it came to bonds, they tried to fake it. At huge cost to their clients.

So, how do you determine your advisor's and broker's expertise and qualifications? What gives these individuals the right to counsel you regarding bond purchases in the new environment? Here are some basic questions you need to ask your broker about the bonds offered to you or already in your portfolio. If he can't answer these questions or cannot do the research needed to find the answers, get a broker who understands the bond market.

What Kind of a Municipal Bond Is It?

This may seem like an elementary question to be glossed over by a naive broker seeking to make a big, fat mark-up. Not so fast. Ask if the municipal bond in question is a revenue bond. Revenue bonds are repaid from the project they were issued to fund—such as a toll road or bridge. Depending on the project, certain revenue bonds can be very safe. For example, revenue bonds that draw their debt service requirement from the revenue of essential services (such as water and sewer projects) are pretty safe. After all, such services are non-discretionary and absolutely must be maintained versus other bond projects whose proceeds are not so important.

Perhaps they're general obligation bonds (GOs). General obligation bonds are repaid from the general fund of the issuer. If the issuer runs short of cash, it has the ability to hike taxes to repay bondholders. Again, pretty safe.

Maybe it is a prerefunded bond. We'll consider these in depth later. For now, just know that other bonds have already been issued to replace the first bonds. The second bond's proceeds are put in a safe escrow account and will be used to repay the first bonds when the time comes. That's why they're known as prerefunded bonds. These are among the safest investment vehicles you can buy if they are escrowed with Treasuries. That way, the municipalities cannot get their greedy little hands on the bond refund escrow account.

If the broker offers a highway bond, ask if it's a GARVEE bond. Grant Anticipation Revenue Vehicles (GARVEE) bonds are tax-exempt. They are backed by annual federal appropriations for federal-aid transportation projects. Such federal backstopping makes GARVEE bonds another reliable fixed income instrument for your portfolio.

Last, ask the broker if the bond he is offering you carries a double-barreled protection from default. These municipal bonds were first introduced in Chapter 1. They are a type of general obligation bond, safer than ordinary general obligation bonds because the sources of repayment are guaranteed by two separate and distinct revenue streams.

What's the Issue Size?

The size of a bond issue determines your liquidity. If the issue is too small, chances are that just a few own it. Few owners means the issue doesn't enjoy a wide market. If you get a bid to sell a small issue bond, it will be at the buyer's price rather than yours. The attitude of such buyers is, "I'm the only game in town. Hit my bid or leave it."

When Was the Bond Last Traded?

It's important to know the trading history of any bond you're considering. The history should include when it traded and at what prices. If your target bond hasn't traded in six months, then something is wrong. Perhaps the issue is too small and doesn't have a big enough market. Or perhaps the bond issuer is such a good quality company or municipality that the bondholders have no interest in selling at any price. Whatever the reason, you want to see an actively traded market—one that trades in your size or larger should you wish to exit.

Are There Any Interest Rate Swaps Involved in the Issue?

Interest rate swaps are a form of derivative security. They have been the death of so many bond investors. Wall Street bankers lured municipal bond officials into these derivatives, which they called interest rate swaps. The most frequently used swaps locked in fixed borrowing costs on variable rate debt. As the economy swooned, local municipalities were horrified to find their bond interest payments tripled or quadrupled due to these toxic swaps. To entice naive issuers into these ill-advised deals, Wall Street managers gave many small school districts cash payments up front. They snapped it up like a dog grabbing a favorite bone. Now they are in danger of defaulting on their bonds with interest rate swaps in them. The bond prices have plummeted.

The Municipal Securities Rulemaking Board refused to create rules regarding the use of derivatives by municipalities. The MSRB is supposed to regulate and supervise the municipal bond market. It did nothing. Christopher Taylor, who was the MSRB Executive Director from 1978 to 2007, admitted that his board wouldn't allow the group to set rules on swaps and derivatives. The investing public can only speculate on why our regulators refused to do their jobs. Some believe it's because whistle blowers don't get hired. The regulators themselves want to work for the same Wall Street bankers they oversee when their tenure in public service is finished. Others speculate it's because the MSRB gets much of its funding from its members—the very Wall Street investment banks they regulate. So why should they make life difficult for these generous members?

Ask your broker if the bond you are interested in has one or more interest rate swap contracts on it. He can find out simply by punching it up on his Bloomberg machine and reading the current news. Alternatively, you can find out yourself. Go on the Web to www.emma.msrb.org. Punch in the CUSIP number of the bond in question and read its Official Statement. Buried among the legalese will be a section on interest rate swaps. If it has interest rate swaps in it, do not buy the bond regardless of the yield.

 Action Step: Interest Rate Swap Contracts

Interest rate swap contracts are to bonds as the red lights and bells warning traffic away are to a railroad crossing. If you buy that bond and try to beat the oncoming train, you'll likely get whacked.

What Is the Debt Coverage?

Our mission is not to make accountants out of you. However, there is one critical number you want to know before buying a bond. That is the debt service coverage ratio. It tells you how much excess net income the bond issuer has over and above all debt service obligations. Essentially, it is a margin of error. For example, debt coverage of 5 times means that net income could drastically fall and the bond issuer would still be able to make its bond payments. On the other hand, an issuer with a debt coverage of just 2 or less might be hard pressed to come up with the cash should things go south. If that happens, then the bond price would fall out of bed and with it, the value of your investment. Further, debt coverage is a moving target. It can change quickly, especially if the economy hits the skids. So you need to constantly update your computations.

Here's the equation used to compute the debt service coverage:

Debt service coverage = (Operating revenue − operating expenses
+ depreciation) ÷ Annual principal and interest payments

Always Use at Least Two Brokers

Many investors feel disloyal to their long-standing broker if they bring in one or more other brokers to supplement their trades. Get over it. This is business, and there's a lot of your hard-earned money on the line here. If you want a best friend, get yourself a Labrador Retriever. They're less expensive than just one bad trade anyway.

No matter how good your primary broker may be, you need a relationship with more than just one brokerage firm. With the financial industry consolidation, there are fewer brokers in the markets, fewer trading desks, and less capital committed to bond inventories. There is also an increased emphasis in marking up bonds to the individual investor's detriment.

Never Buy Bonds Online

Never, ever. Don't do it. Pointing and clicking to buy stocks is very different than pointing and clicking to buy bonds. With stocks, everyone sees the prices in real time. That's not the case for bonds. The online bond platforms provided to individual investors by the brokerage industry—Schwab, Vanguard, Fidelity, TD Ameritrade, and all the others—are fed by numerous broker dealers. Each takes a piece of the price for itself. By the time the price is quoted to a retail investor, the mark-up is way, way off the market.

Instead, use several qualified broker/dealers with whom you have ongoing relationships. Make them bid against one another for your business. This allows you to negotiate and to gain insight from their minute-by-minute participation in the bond market.

No Discount Bond Brokers

Just because you deal with a discount securities broker does not mean he is discounting their execution prices for bond trades. Bonds, unlike stocks, do not have a real-time price. Instead, your broker/dealer feeds the trades into the TRACE system within fifteen minutes of execution. TRACE is the bond tracking system developed by the Financial Industry Regulatory Authority (FINRA). It shows where bonds have traded and when. The bond broker can hold your trade within this 15-minute window until he has posted the purchase of the bond he is selling to you. This may be at a significant discount from where you are buying it. That discount is the broker's mark-up. Unlike a trade execution fee for stocks, the broker's compensation is included in their mark-up. No matter what your discount broker may say about there being no bond execution fees, he is making a handsome profit on each trade through the price mark-up.

Look at Your Portfolio as a Whole

That's the way we professionals look at clients' portfolios. The securities in an investment portfolio are not a series of independent purchases. Rather, the portfolio is a congruent team of different players with different capabilities and missions working together to produce a targeted result.

Before the credit crisis, those investors who thought of their portfolio as a series of independent purchases used to buy bonds just based on yield. Before the credit crisis, the sectors they bought were financials and autos. Of course they did, because these two were the biggest bond issuers and had the highest yields. They loaded up their portfolio with these two sectors, creating an undue concentration of risk in just two industries.

Then the credit crisis hit. It slammed into the financials and autos like a freight train running a crossing. These same investors discovered they were way overallocated to these sectors that were so vulnerable. They had the worst portfolio losses compared to those with a more balanced portfolio.

 Action Step: Undue Concentration

Fix any undue concentrations of your portfolio that could severely damage overall performance if the issuer, industry, or geographic area suffered. Populate your investment portfolio with a balance of bonds whose maturities, issuers, types, and repayment sources are diversified. The goal is to win the entire war, not just one battle.

Equity investors have always distributed their portfolios into diversified industry groups. Fixed income investors must now follow their lead or get crushed by the changing rules of engagement. This is true not just for corporate bonds. Municipal bonds can suffer from downturns in particular areas, too. For example, say you are offered a water revenue bond for a new housing development in Stockton, California, where the foreclosure rate is high. Not a good idea.

First of all, that bond depends on property owners from a new housing development paying their water bills. What happens if residential sales in the development are way under the level needed to service the bond and foreclosures ratchet even higher? How can you tell? In this case, all you had to do was look at the real estate sales and foreclosure statistics for that area. Stockton was growing very fast. That would have been a good thing had the buyers not been speculators looking to flip these new residential units and others who were taking out subprime loans to buy a house whose price was way over their heads. When the real estate market turned upside down, the entire area went down with it.

Stockton anticipates budget deficits to run $30 million. Worse still, 77 percent of Stockton's revenues go to pay police and firefighters. Sales and property taxes are way down as home prices decline 60 percent. Finally, unemployment is 16 percent. Saying these bonds have a problem is an understatement.

Modeling your bond portfolio is a matter of common sense. Think of what can go wrong, and then carry the thought to its ultimate impact on your bond repayment.

 Action Step: New Issue Market

Always try to buy your municipal bonds on the new issue market. This is the only time you're getting the right price and same price as other investors.

Beware the Government

The U.S. government is still finding its way through the economic and credit crisis. It has involved itself in industries no one ever thought it would. The student loan agency Sallie Mae is a prime example. The government decided to issue student loans directly rather than through Sallie Mae, the agency specifically set up for this purpose. Overnight, Sallie Mae was scrambling to reinvent itself. The bondholders were left holding the bag, wondering what hit them.

The government also seized control over the bankruptcy of General Motors. They shoved the bondholders out of their seniority position in the capital structure. In the bondholders' place it put the auto workers' union (composed of hundreds of thousands of voters). This move cost the bondholders most of their stake in GM, about $27 billion. It was contrary to contract law.

The free markets once never had to worry about the U.S. government's footprint or interference in their business. Now potential governmental intervention or interference is a consideration in every bond investment made. Before you buy any bond, assess how the government will react and possibly overreach its constitutionally granted powers. If the worst case seems possible, pass on the investment.

Never Trust the Rating Agencies or the Insurers

The bond rating agencies get their fees from the very companies and municipalities they rate. They have essentially sold their ratings to the highest bidders. AIG, one of the largest bond insurance agencies, continued to flaunt its AAA rating just weeks before it admitted it lacked sufficient funds to honor the enormous potential claims resulting from its credit default swaps. There are many such stories in the monoline bond insurance industry. Now the insurers are so far overextended in their promises that most cannot honor all their liabilities. Only a handful carry any sort of credible rating.

Don't trust the insured rating of any issuer whose bonds you are considering. Instead, look to the underlying rating usually attached. This is a rating stripped of any bond insurance. It rates the issuer's financial capacity on its own. If this rating meets your requirements, then proceed.

Bail Out on a Leveraged Buyout

Leveraged buyouts (LBOs) by private equity firms require the acquired companies to issue huge amounts of debt to fund the private equity purchase and get their money out. This puts the target company's original bondholders in tremendous jeopardy. Suddenly, the balance sheet is bloated by this new debt that does nothing more than put money in the private equity firm's pocket. Worse, this new debt is most likely senior to yours on the capital structure. Your credit metrics (see Chapter 11, Bond Analysis) will deteriorate faster than a speeding bullet.

LBOs are the doomsday scenario for existing bondholders of the acquired companies. If you own corporate bonds in such a company, get out as fast as you can. Any time we have waited to sell because we didn't think the takeover would happen, we were sorry. Get out the moment you hear your company is in play. Better to be safe than sorry. As witness, observe the carnage to once-good companies the last LBO frenzy caused: First Data, Harrah's, Cablevision, Univision, the list goes on. The corporate bond junk pile is littered with catastrophic deals gone sour. Don't let it happen to you.

Recognize Increasing Complexity

Managing a bond portfolio whose income you need has increased in difficulty and in the levels of complexity. No longer can pensioners lay their bonds away thinking they are safe. It takes time and imagination to deal with all of the assessment tools and to consider what can go wrong to jeopardize your holdings. If you are not up to this task, then hire a professional to do it for you.

Out of misguided pride and being a little penny wise, we know several investors who insisted on doing it themselves. They had been managing their own investments for 30 and 40 years. But not in a climate like we have now. They didn't want to spend the $5,000 annual fee a professional money manager would charge for their $1 million portfolio. Instead, they wound up losing a large portion of their portfolio.

The *purpose-driven* investor is out for three things regarding his investments: safety, liquidity, and yield in that order. The intent is to build a fortress surrounding his holdings—a fortress designed to withstand shifts in the economy and decisions by the government that are adverse to public policy. Chapter 3 shows how to create a program of fortress investing.

3

Fortress Investing

Imagine a medieval fortress like the one shown here. Formidable, isn't it? Even before intruders can get to the sheer castle walls rising vertically out of the earth, they must scale the surrounding ramparts. A daunting task. There's probably a moat somewhere that must be crossed. Of course, then intruders must deal with the drawbridge—every impregnable fortress needs a drawbridge. The occupants are safe inside. Nothing can get to them without their knowledge or permission.

That's the same figurative fortress we want to build around our portfolios. The fortress protecting your investments must withstand all sorts of assaults. Make no mistake, these will surely come. They will range from our government's seeking to redistribute America's wealth from those who earned it to those who can't; to incompetent CEOs of companies and municipalities in which you have an interest; to crooked money managers and brokers; to regulatory bodies that do nothing but protect Wall Street's own interests; and to adverse economic and interest rate changes. No matter what the future brings, the fortress surrounding your investment portfolio must withstand assaults from all comers. Sure, any given assault may sting and even cause some damage. But it won't bring down the entire castle.

This chapter shows what insiders already know and what you must incorporate into your fixed income investment discipline. The Action Steps spell out the changes you must make to shore up your castle walls against the slings and arrows of a not-so-nice world. This is not rocket science. Most rules of fortress investing are commonsense.

Impregnable Fortress

Make them second nature. Include them on your pre-investment checklist that you always consult before pulling the trigger on a buy decision.

Diversified Construction Materials

Just as an impenetrable castle is built from a variety of tough materials, so is a safe investment portfolio. We accomplish this by taking a diversified approach to what goes into the investment portfolio. We'll build our investment fortress with enough different bonds that can weather any onslaught. These must be bonds that you want to own regardless of what might happen.

Different Names Aren't Enough

Before the 2008 credit crisis, investors thought they were diversified by owning a lot of different-named corporate bonds. They got whacked just as if their entire net worth was in a single name. Yes, they owned bonds issued by Citigroup, Bank of America, and General Electric. However, they failed to consider that each of these was handcuffed to the financial industry. When financials crumbled, so did their portfolio.

These investors had reasoned, "Yes, we're concentrated in a single industry. But these companies are too big to fail. We're safe." Too many people shared that view. They thought the biggies such as Citi, BOA, Fannie Mae and Freddie Mac, Morgan Stanley, Bear Stearns, and Lehman Brothers all were too big to get into any real trouble. They weren't.

The next worst thing to actually failing happened. The U.S. government gained entrance to the castle. It didn't use a battering ram or any sort of siege engine. Instead, it waltzed right through the gates using TARP money as their ticket to the inner sanctum. The billions it offered bought it the right to usurp management. It hired and fired CEOs and directors. It made a show of ordering up business plans and then insisted they were wrong.

When the Chrysler and GM bondholders objected to the deal the government gave them, the government did the unthinkable. It spit in the bondholders' faces. It replaced the bondholder's' senior credit positions with common stock that not only was worth a fraction of their bond holdings, but it was last in the food chain of bankruptcy repayment. The bondholders of Chrysler and, General Motors and preferred shareholders of Freddie Mac and those of Fannie Mae suddenly found themselves on the outside looking in.

 Action Step: Diversity in Name Only

Diversity in names is not enough. Structure diversity of the industries and geographic regions represented in your bond portfolio. Limit exposure to any one industry or region to no more than 15 percent of the entire pool of funds.

It's All About the Capital Structure

The capital structure is the ownership of a corporation. Corporate bond-holders must know just where they stand in the capital structure in case the enterprise encounters economic troubles. Certainly, bondholders enjoy a senior position to shareholders of common stock. However, debt has various degrees of payment seniority.

Stay at the senior end of the corporate capitalization structure. Senior secured notes stand farther up the line than do unsecured subordinated notes.

Movement Within the Capital Structure

Many companies have initiated stock buy-back programs and de-leveraging initiatives. The effects are usually opposite one another. Stock buy-back programs are often financed by bond issues. Management reduces the pool of outstanding stock. This often causes the stock price to rise. For top management seeking to exercise their stock options without drawing undue attention, such a program will allow the stock price to remain stable as so many new shares hit the market.

The problem for existing bondholders is that management just added hugely to the company's debt burden without getting anything of equal or greater value in exchange to repay this new debt. Companies that have done this include General Electric, Merrill Lynch, AIG Insurance, and Washington Mutual. The risk is that the margin of error just shrank. With it, the debt coverage fell. The risk associated with holding such companies' bonds rose. The more senior your bond on the capital structure, the better, just in case they can't climb out of this new debt burden.

Maturity Distributions

Whether a corporate or a municipal bond, the capital structure probably has a number of debt maturities. The key for bondholders is to avoid taking a position at the back of the line. Should things worsen, there will be less cash available with which to pay bondholders.

Figure 3.1 shows a distribution chart of debt maturities for Dell, Inc. Notice the time spacing between the various maturities:

Investors would probably not want to be much further out on the maturity distribution than 2014 or 2019.

 Action Step: Picking Your Maturity Position

Be very aware of your corporate bond's position on the debt maturity distribution. If it is too far out, the company may use all its cash paying other debt issues and could run short by the time your bond comes due. Instead, stay senior in the capitalization structure.

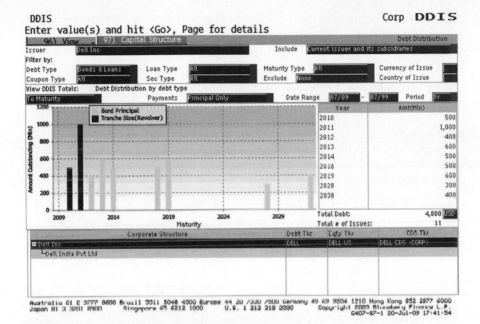

Figure 3.1   Debt Maturity Distribution

Defining and Following the Rules

The fortress of prudence and judgment surrounding your bond portfolio consists of several specific rules to follow. These are simple to understand. Most revolve around imagining what can go wrong and what and whom to protect against. By nature, bond investors are pessimists. We are constantly looking over our shoulders to see what lurks out there that could damage the portfolio.

What Can the Government Do?

If a company or industry truly is too big or too important to fail, then the government could try saving it. This proved disastrous for the bondholders of GM and Chrysler. The government gave the GM employee trust fund (actually, the United Auto Workers) a 17.5 percent stake and $6.5 billion in a new issue of preferred stock that pays 9 percent annually. That's $585 million each year in income. The government forced bondholders to eat a $17 billion discount on their holdings. This is the type of lopsided shared sacrifice bond investors must anticipate when dealing with the government. The next industry on the government's hit list could be healthcare or insurance.

The first question you must ask is what could the government do to the company, industry, or municipality that would cause the bond to lose value? Since bonds have maturity and call dates, these time frames form a bracket around the timing of any adverse government action.

How Liquid Is This Corporate Bond?

Should something occur on the horizon that you don't like, you must have the ability to get out of the bond position. Liquidity equates to the size of the issue. A good guideline to use when judging an appropriate issue size is that it should be at least $250 million with $500 million as optimal.

 Action Step: Don't Always Equate Size to Liquidity

During the height of the credit crisis, even the largest bonds issues proved illiquid. Investors needing to get out couldn't get bids. The brokerage firms weren't allocating capital to bond inventory. They were simply matching buyers to sellers—of which most were sellers with very few buyers.

Is the Existing Debt Manageable?

Simply put, does the issuer have the ability to service this debt? Take a look at its balance sheet. How much cash does it have? Ask yourself, what are the components of current assets? Are they easily sold if necessary? What about current liabilities? Finally, how much greater are the current assets than the current liabilities? Take a look at the sample balance sheet in Table 3.1.

In this case, cash is at a reasonable level of $407MM. Receivables and inventory make up the lion's share of current assets. These are quickly converted to cash if need be. The liabilities are not unusual with payables and other short-term liabilities being the largest components. Finally, current assets are 196 percent of current liabilities

Table 3.1   A current section of balance sheet

Assets	
+ Cash & Near Cash Items	407.20
+ Short-Term Investments	0.00
+ Accounts & Notes Receivable	697.00
+ Inventories	605.60
+ Other Current Assets	281.50
Total Current Assets	**1,991.30**
Liabilities & Shareholders' Equity	
+ Accounts Payable	501.10
+ Short-Term Borrowings	74.60
+ Other Short-Term Liabilities	439.40
Total Current Liabilities	**1,015.10**

($1,991.30 ÷ $1015.10 — 196%). That's a little low. Look more closely at how this company compares with others in its class. Are revenues and expenses stable? Make a judgment regarding its overall financial strength.

Management Stability

We want some assurance that management knows what it is doing. Take a look at the senior executive's' backgrounds and tenure at the company or municipality. You don't want to own a revolving door for management. Citigroup's bondholders were concerned when Sandy Weil named attorney Charles Prince his successor. Prince had no experience running one of the world's largest financial institutions. It turned out the bondholders had reason for their worry. Citigroup imploded under Prince's watch.

You also want to know that management is friendly toward the bondholders. For example, a management that funds its stock buy-back program with a bond issue is not particularly bondholder friendly. To the four companies mentioned earlier we add Macy's, Home Depot, CBS, Gannett, Lincoln National, Hartford Financial, GE, and Merrill Lynch. All the new debt provides is a temporary up tick for stockholders. Management gets to exercise its stock options. The underwriters have the chance they've been waiting for to unload their stock at a profit.

Bondholders look for a management that cares about its balance sheet and current ratio. We want to know that the CEO and Board won't issue debt or spend cash just for the short term—but looks to the long-term good of the company. Additionally, we don't want a management that makes acquisitions at the top of the market by issuing debt as Rio Tinto did when it bought Alcan Aluminum.

Action Step: Don't Equate Company Size to Management Capabilities

Sometimes the highest paid executives make the biggest, most costly mistakes. Be careful of the emperor—too often he doesn't have any clothes on and those close to him are too afraid for their jobs to say so.

John Thain kept assuring Wall Street that Merrill Lynch was adequately capitalized to absorb losses in collateralized mortgage obligations (CMOs), subprime mortgages, derivatives, and CDOs. His lieutenants were either too afraid for their jobs to correct him or were equally oblivious. In fact, Thain didn't have a clue what Merrill's losses and liabilities would be. As a result, he had to sell the firm in what turned out to be a rescue operation. Billed as the Great White Hope for Merrill, he turned out to be quite the opposite.

Assessing management is the most difficult lesson to learn. The bonds issued by unstable management often have a higher yield than others. The reason: There's a rate for every risk. The risk of buying an unstable management team is greater than buying a management that is more experienced and savvy.

Positive Cash Flow

For corporate bonds we want to know that not only is the company profitable but that it has a positive cash flow. If cash drains every month with no apparent way of stanching the tide, then it's only a matter of time before bondholders have a default on their hands.

Cash flow should be adequate to repay upcoming obligations. For us bondholders, the most important obligations are the bonds we hold. We introduced the bond maturity chart earlier. Look at the maturity distribution for Thermo Fisher Scientific 6.125% due July 1, 2015 (see Figure 3.2). The issue size is $500MM. There isn't much in front of that maturity to compete for cash. Therefore, we're

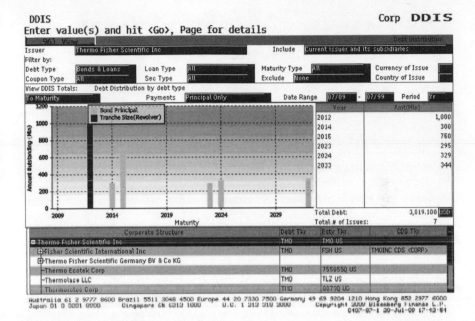

Figure 3.2 Fisher Maturity Chart

Source: Bloomberg Finance L.P. © 2009 Bloomberg Finance L.P. All rights reserved. Used with permission.

comfortable that Thermo Fisher can repay our bonds when they come due in 2015.

Ability to Refinance

Access to the credit markets is essential when evaluating a company. The bonds we buy cannot be the last credit this company will ever be granted. Likewise, we want our company to refinance its debt should interest rates decline. This works in both the company's favor as well as for us bondholders.

Stable Revenue Stream

Just as we look for a stable management team, so too do we look for stable revenue. Companies that issue bonds should not be hugely subject to market swings and events outside their control. Form a judgment as to the vulnerability of the company's or municipality's revenue stream.

Action Step: Size Does Not Equate to Stability

The bigger they are, sometimes the harder they fall. This can tip the scales against your portfolio. Chrysler and General Motors are just two examples.

Investors soon discovered that GE earnings were driven by its subsidiary, GE Capital. But GE Capital was nothing more than a hedge fund in drag. Bad news when the 2008 credit crisis hit. GE Capital couldn't get credit to fund its business. GE Capital, and ultimately GE, was the same house of cards as the other highly levered hedge funds. This debacle has so far cost the bondholders who sold out billions.

Compartmentalize Risk

Be aware of and manage the two most significant types of risk associated with fixed income investing:

1. Asset allocation risk
2. Money manager risk

Asset Allocation Risk

Asset allocation has just three easily implemented risk-limiting strategies. First is allocation in a single industry group. Limit exposure to any single industry for corporates or geographic region for municipal bonds to about 15 percent of the bond portfolio. Second, within an industry group or geographic region, limit exposure to any single name to 3 to 5 percent of the portfolio. Third, allocate no more than 20 percent of the portfolio to a single maturity year. This reduces reinvestment risk.

These three simple rules serve to compartmentalize damage in the event of an attack on the fortress.

Money Manager Risk

You've probably been Bernie Maddoff'd to death. However, his inexcusable excesses provide a perfect example of what not to do if you chose to hire a money manager for your fixed income investments.

Hire only managers that domicile your money and securities at a reputable third party custodian—such as Fidelity, Schwab, or JP Morgan. These companies will hold your cash and securities for you. The money manager cannot get his hands on it. All statements go to you without the opportunity for doctoring by the manager.

Action Step: Keep a Distance from Your Money Manager

Never, ever write a check for an investment directly to and in the name of a money manager. All monies should be paid directly to the third party custodian.

The statement depicted in Figure 3.3 was pulled from documents of Bernie Madoff's management company. What's wrong with this document? It looks credible and official, doesn't it? The problem is that it's Madoff's own firm that produced the statement. Investors had only Bernie's word that their accounts had in them what he said

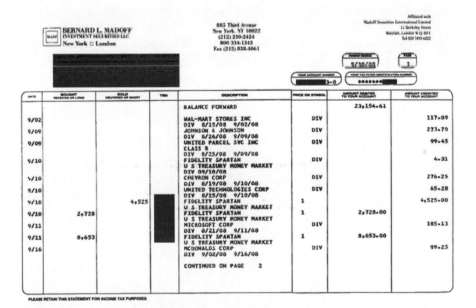

Figure 3.3   Madoff statement

they had. In Madoff's case, there was no third party custodian of client funds.

Next, insist on seeing the custodian's audited financial statements prepared and attested to by a reputable independent public accounting firm. This is more of a credibility check than anything else. The custodian firm should have the ability to hire a reputable auditing firm. Not only did Madoff act as his own custodian but also his personal CPA—also a Madoff client—issued the opinion on Madoff's financial statements.

There's another, more hidden risk. Let's say that you have done your homework on a money manager. He's reputable. He uses a third party custodian. He never asked for checks written directly to him. He has the custodian send you the audited financial statements, trade confirmations, and account statements. So far, so good.

There's still a potential problem. Your money manager is charged with exercising professional due diligence in all investment transactions he does on your behalf. Except not all of them do. Bernie Madoff received almost half of the $58 billion of investor money he lost from feeder managers. These are money managers who feed their own client monies to other money managers (presumably more skilled) to invest.

In some cases, these feeder managers had billions on account with Madoff. They never thought twice that Madoff didn't use a third party custodian for client money. They never bothered to find out who Madoff's auditor was. In fact, simply driving by the address on the CPA's letterhead would have revealed nothing more than a small storefront address. Certainly not the type of accounting firm equipped to audit one of the country's largest, seemingly most successful money management firms.

The feeders didn't do any of the most basic due diligence. They just sent their clients' money to Bernie, never to be seen again. They received a handsome fee from Bernie on top of their management fee from the clients. They forgot the cardinal rule of investing: There's a rate for every risk. Above market rates guarantee above market risk. There are no exceptions to this rule. Ever. Madoff was giving (claiming to give, actually) above-market returns year after year. Yet he published no clearly defined trading discipline. No one knew how he did it. He didn't.

When interviewed, some of these feeders admitted to wondering about Bernie. When asked why they didn't pull their client's' money out, they said they liked the return. There's another rule they failed to follow: *When in doubt, get out.*

The Essential Prime Broker

Prime broker is a designation given a client by its custodian firm. It has to do with the size of its accounts. Being designated a prime broker account allows your money manager to use any broker outside the custodian's firm he wishes to execute any particular trade. This is called trading away, for which the custodian charges a small fee for each transaction (the trade away fee). If you've hired a smart manager, he'll more than make up those fees by buying and selling at significantly better prices than you can obtain on your own. Trade away fees can be $15 to $50 per transaction. Your money manager has already negotiated a flat fee with the custodian firm. Trade away fees over $50 are outrageous. You can and should negotiate them downward.

Being a prime broker account ensures that your money managers have complete freedom to get the best price for your trade. Without it, your money manager is forced to use only the custodian's trading desk. He cannot possibly get a competitive price for your bond trades. Further, non-prime brokers pretty much buy at retail level—the same as you can. What's the benefit of hiring a money manager who cannot get better trades than you could yourself?

Diversifying the Broker's Brokers

Every money manager designated as a prime broker uses institutional brokers to execute his trades. The question is how many such institutional brokers does the broker or money manager do business with? Every professional has his own number. Ours is at least twelve. Such diversity of the institutional brokers used ensures access to most any bond you could want and a healthy competition to get you the best price.

Whatever the number of institutional brokers used, ask who they are. Most reputable brokers and money managers use a combination of the very large wire houses and regionals.

Coming up in Chapter 4 you will peer into how the bond market functions sometimes for you but often against you if you don't know the rules.

CHAPTER 4

Bond Execution

There's a reason why they call it execution: Retail bond investors who simply accept the bond broker's price in the secondary market without question usually get their heads handed to them. Unlike the stock market, bond prices are not posted on a regulated exchange. It is a telephone market where brokers talk with clients and with one another, haggling over price until they reach an agreement.

Let's assume you've done your homework, evaluated the political, economic, and business climates surrounding your bond, and have decided to take the plunge. Your broker may already have the bond in his firm's inventory. In that case, he knows just what he paid for it. A quick look at his Bloomberg machine tells him where it's currently trading, when it traded, and what kind of customer bought or sold it (institutional or retail). At this point the broker knows much more about the value of that bond than you do. Now the only thing in question is how much of a mark-up does the brokerage firm and the retail broker wish to take? Then he'll have his price.

If the broker doesn't have your bond in his firm's inventory, he must have the trader "work the order." That is, the trader must call his buddies at other bond brokerage firms and bond dealers to get it. They will negotiate a wholesale price between their two firms. Once the trader has the bond, he marks up the price to the retail broker. The retail broker—that would be *your* retail broker—marks up the price again and then offers you the bond. All the while, every mark-up reduces your yield.

The mechanics of bond trading are not difficult. Bond trading is a contact sport—it does involve talking and negotiating with your broker. It also requires you to be informed about the bond, its trading and price history, and its relative risk. You will be pleasantly surprised at how much information is available about most any bond you want with just a little digging.

TRACE-ing the Trading History

You could ask your broker to look on his Bloomberg machine for the most recent prices of your bond and what size and kind of transactions they were. If your broker doesn't have a Bloomberg machine, then he's not active in the bond market. Find someone who maintains an operational presence in Bondland. However, asking your broker for recent prices is like asking a used car salesman how much others have paid for the same car you want to buy. You may not always get the real answer.

There's a better way than asking the person looking to make as much money for himself as he can from your bond trade. You can visit the Municipal Securities Rulemaking Board's web site, www.investinginbonds.com. This is the TRACE Reporting System introduced in Chapter 2. It provides similar information to what your broker sees on his Bloomberg machine. Just enter the CUSIP number of the bond in which you are interested. Up pops a screen showing the trading history by date, size traded, and price. A graphical analysis shows you where prices are trending. A bond calculator shows you current yield, annual yield, yield-to-maturity, and the bond's cash flows by month and year.

This wealth of information will help you negotiate a fair price for the bond. You can see where the market is for your bond. If your broker offers you a price off the market, you now have the information to correct him and to make an informed counter offer. Such information levels the playing field between individual investors and their brokers. Of course, the brokers have not embraced the investing public's access to the TRACE reporting system because it reduces their advantage and their income.

Figure 4.1 shows an example of how to use the TRACE system. Look at the figure, which shows the disparity between prices of the same bond traded:

This isn't some esoteric, weird bond. It is American Express 5.875% due May 2013—an investment-grade corporate bond. There are a number of transactions occurring at 100.250, whereas the

AXP 5 ⅞ 05/13 $ ↑ **100.250** **+2.321**   Corp **QRD**
At 12:30   Vol 6,485   Op 95.500   Hi 100.250   Lo 95.500   Prev 97.929   TRMT

| Definitions | QR/QRM Options | | Multi-Day Quote Recap | Page 2 |

Time 08:00:00 To 17:30:00 Min Vol(M)▮▮▮▮   Source TRAC   USD
Date 5/22 To 5/29 Price Range ▮▮▮▮ To ▮▮▮▮ Sprd To 🅑 Benchmark
AMER EXPRESS CR   AXP5 ⅞ 05/02/13   100.010/100.010   (5.87/5.87) TRAC

Date	Time	Act	Price	Ind	Yield	RPS	Sprd	Benchmark	Size(M)	CC	Trd Time	Date
05/29	11:59:49		↑99.774		5.939	S	356 6	T1 ⅞ 04/30/14	15		11:59:45	5/29/09
05/29	11:55:14		99.655		5.973	D	359.9	T1 ⅞ 04/30/14	10		11:55:00	5/29/09
05/29	11:55:06		↑99.655		5.973	S	359.9	T1 ⅞ 04/30/14	10		11:55:04	5/29/09
05/29	11:43:17		99.026		6.157	S	380.1	T1 ⅞ 04/30/14	200		11:41:43	5/29/09
05/29	11:39:52		↓99.026		6.157	S	379.1	T1 ⅞ 04/30/14	200		11:27:00	5/29/09
05/29	11:23:41		↑100.250		5.801	S	343.8	T1 ⅞ 04/30/14	25		11:23:00	5/29/09
05/29	11:19:19		97.098		6.729	B	435.9	T1 ⅞ 04/30/14	2		11:19:00	5/29/09
05/29	11:19:19		↓97.098		6.729	D	435.9	T1 ⅞ 04/30/14	2		11:19:00	5/29/09
05/29	11:19:06	X	↓97.098		6.729	B	435.7	T1 ⅞ 04/30/14	2	*X	11:18:00	5/29/09
05/29	11:19:06	X	↓97.098		6.729	D	435.7	T1 ⅞ 04/30/14	2	*X	11:18:00	6/20/00
05/29	11:11:27		99.180		6.112	S	373.6	T1 ⅞ 04/30/14	250		11:11:21	5/29/09
05/29	11:11:06		↓99.180		6.112	S	374.1	T1 ⅞ 04/30/14	250		11:10:59	5/29/09
05/29	11:08:22		↑100.250		5.801	S	343.0	T1 ⅞ 04/30/14	50		11:08:00	5/29/09
05/29	11:01:49		↓98.692		6.255	D	387.2	T1 ⅞ 04/30/14	485		11:01:44	5/29/09
05/29	10:59:57		100.250		5.801	S	340.9	T1 ⅞ 04/30/14	26		10:59:00	5/29/09
05/29	10:59:44		↑100.250		5.801	S	340.9	T1 ⅞ 04/30/14	25		10:59:00	5/29/09
05/29	10:54:20		↓100.700		5.950	C	350.0	T1 ⅞ 04/30/14	20		10:54:15	5/29/09
05/29	10:49:59		100.250		5.801	S	341.3	T1 ⅞ 04/30/14	100		10:49:00	6/20/00

Australia 61 2 9777 8600 Brazil 5511 3048 4500 Europe 44 20 7330 7500 Germany 49 69 9204 1210 Hong Kong 852 2977 6000
Japan 81 3 3201 8900   Singapore 65 6212 1000   U.S. 1 212 318 2000   Copyright 2009 Bloomberg Finance L.P.
G366-87-0 29-Mau-09 13:44:16

Figure 4.1   TRACE System Price Differences

market actually appears to be closer to 99.026. These retail buyers and retail sellers weren't looking at the TRACE system before they acted. Naughty, naughty. They will be sorry.

 Action Step: Importance of Using TRACE

Never pull the trigger on a bond trade without first consulting the TRACE system at www.investinginbonds.com. This tells you the trading and price history—indispensable information you need when negotiating with your broker.

We bond professionals who manage other people's money for a living use TRACE as a price reference for each and every bond trade, every day, all day. No professional can manage portfolios without using TRACE.

Pricing the New Issue Muni Market

Action Step: Buy New Issues Whenever Possible

Buy municipal bonds in the new issue market whenever possible.

The new issue municipal bond market is the only time individual investors are guaranteed they paid the same price as the large institutional investors. Every investor is equal in the eyes of the new issue market. There's even an added incentive for individual investors: You get a one- or two-day head start before the institutions are allowed to place their orders. This is called the *retail order period*. It is the only time the little guys get a break in the municipal bond market. So seize the advantage.

Action Step: Get on the New Issue List

Tell your broker that you want him to show you every new municipal bond issue that has a retail order period. If he's with a big brokerage firm with access to the retail order periods of new muni issues, he has a list of clients with the same request. He'll be glad to add you to his e-mail list. When he sells the bond he gets a concession fee without doing much work.

Generally, the larger firms such as Morgan Stanley, Citigroup, or JP Morgan have more access to new issues and retail order periods than small broker/dealers or the discount houses. Brokers and money managers whose trading volume does not qualify them for prime broker status generally do not participate in retail order periods. This is yet another reason to use several brokers, at least one of which is a large institution.

Trade Confirmations

These are the litmus tests that your broker and money manager are acting as you directed them to. The trade confirmations and account statements must come directly (and unopened, either hard copy or electronically) to you from the third party custodian of your money and securities. As a courtesy, most will also send a copy to your accountant, trustee, or other designated parties to the account.

Resist Complacency

Trade confirmations are mailed the next day after the trade is made. They provide a much faster recording of your account's transactions than does the account statement the broker/dealer provides at month end. Your responsibility is to verify that each trade complies with the parameters agreed to with your broker or money manager. If not, then insist on an immediate correction from your broker or money manager.

Problems are usually nothing more than errors. Some trades fail. Deposits can be placed in the wrong account. Distribution of bond interest payments or proceeds from bond maturities or liquidation can be delayed or misrouted to the wrong account. It happens. Your responsibility is to find such mistakes and bring them to your broker's attention for correction.

Money managers automatically reconcile trades, cash in and cash out. Don't rely on your broker to do this for you. Your money is more important to you than to him since he probably has at least several hundred accounts to look after.

Along with appropriateness of the bond being bought on your behalf, part of your trade confirm review should make sure that your broker or money manager is sprinkling your trades among a number of firms rather than just one favorite or even his own custodial firm. Why? Using one firm doesn't force price competition among different firms. Without competition, your broker is nothing more than a highly compensated order taker. That's not what you pay him for. If your broker tells you that his prices beat the street in all cases, all the time, it is a lie and an insult. Just one such lie sours the relationship forever. Change brokers or money managers.

Keep up this diligent monitoring for the entire duration of your relationship with your brokers and money managers. They have been known to change things without notice once they think you're not looking. Make sure they know you're looking closely at them.

Managing Money Is Work

Done right, with diligence and thoroughness, managing money is hard work. It's work even if you employ a professional money manager to do it for you. Every broker and money manager needs an overseer. If it's your money, then that is your job. Imagine how thrilled Bernie Madoff's victims would be to get another crack at revisiting the errors they made in neglecting their responsibilities of money management oversight. The few minutes such review takes can save you millions. Do it.

We know of one money manager who understood his clients would object if he didn't use a third party custodian. So he did. He used a big third party custodian. However, he told his clients that the custodian's statements were so convoluted and difficult to understand (often true), prone to errors, and outdated by the time clients receive them (also sometimes true) that they should ignore them. The money manager said that he would provide them a much easier to understand monthly statement that was accurate and took half as long to get to them.

His witless clients did as they were told. They threw away the custodian-produced account statements without even looking at them. He doctored the client's' account balances appearing on his in-house produced statements. The clients lost somewhere near $100 million. By way of explanation, the ersatz money manager proclaimed that no single client lost more than $1 million and that it's not like it was anyone's last million or anything. The money manager never spent a single day in jail. It cost him millions in legal fees (paid from client money, no doubt) to accomplish that feat.

Riding the Yield Curve

Don't just buy a bond because your broker says it's a decent yield. Check on the yields at various maturities. The Treasury yield curve is the common base used in Bondland. Think of it as Bondland's GPS. All other bond yields are a function of the Treasury yield curve. This is called the spread to the Treasury yield curve, or simply, the spread. If we assume that U.S. Treasuries are a sure thing to pay off at maturity and are not likely to skip an interest payment until that time, then the closer a bond's yield to that U.S. Treasury, the closer to that level of risk—essentially no risk. Conversely, the greater the spread off the yield curve, the higher the yield, but also the greater that bond's risk. This again proves there's a rate for every risk.

The trick to riding the yield curve is to execute your bond trades within a spread to the Treasury yield curve that is as close to the

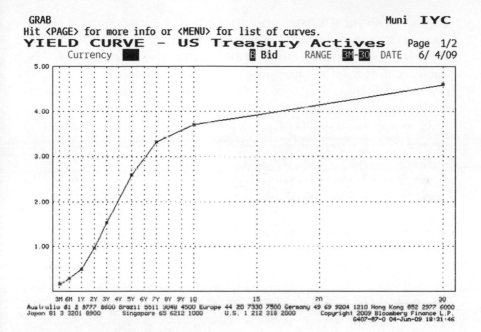

GRAB   Muni **IYC**
Hit <PAGE> for more info or <MENU> for list of curves.
YIELD CURVE – US Treasury Actives Page 1/2
         Currency ▮   ▧ Bid   RANGE ▧▧-▧▧ DATE   6/ 4/09

Australia 61 2 9777 8600 Brazil 5511 3048 4500 Europe 44 20 7330 7500 Germany 49 69 9204 1210 Hong Kong 652 2977 6000
Japan 81 3 3201 8900   Singapore 65 6212 1000   U.S. 1 212 318 2000   Copyright 2009 Bloomberg Finance L.P.
                                                                              G407-87-0 04-Jun-09 18:31:46

Figure 4.2 Treasury Yield Curve

market as possible. For example, if the spread for a bond you want is 45 basis points above the yield curve, then your targeted yield to maturity is the Treasury yield plus 45 basis points. Any price you're presented that is below that yield is too high, and any price above that yield is a bargain.

Be sure you nail the relationship between price and yield. *Price drives yield. The lower the price you pay, the higher the yield. The higher the price you pay, the lower the yield.*

The *Wall Street Journal* prints the Treasury yield curve every day. You can also get it on the Web at www.investinginbonds.com. Figure 4.2 shows what the Treasury yield curve looks like.

As a rule, taxable yields (such as on corporate bonds) are a spread *above* the Treasury yield curve. For example, say we want a five-year corporate bond. The yield curve tells us that five-year Treasuries yield 2 percent. An Alcoa bond due in five years yields 8 percent. That's a whopping 600 basis point spread over the Treasury yield. That huge spread represents the red lights flashing and bells clanging at the railroad crossing. It warns bond investors that Alcoa is much riskier than a Treasury. In fact, Alcoa has a number of challenges. It has a highly leveraged balance sheet in an industry that is in the tank. Not much comfort for bond investors seeking assurance that they will be paid on maturity and the company won't skip any interest payments in between

On the other hand, tax-free yields (such as for municipal bonds) are a percentage of comparable maturing Treasuries—usually 80 to 85 percent. However, at the height of the credit crisis, all yields on municipal bonds exceeded Treasuries by historically high levels. That's testimony to how skittish bond investors were for all bonds, even municipal bonds, after the 2008 credit meltdown. This told bond investors that the municipal bonds with the unusual *positive* spread over the Treasury yield curve were a great bargain because their prices were down.

Checklist for Corporate Bonds

Before you place an order for a corporate bond, there are eight things you need to consider. We've put them in the form of the checklist below. With practice this checklist will become second nature. You'll run through it automatically—like Tiger Woods addressing the golf ball before he pulls the trigger that fires the cannon. Here are the checklist items to resolve about any corporate bond you are considering:

Corporate Bond Checklist
1. **Diversification:** Does the industry and business of this company help diversify your bond portfolio?
2. **Credit quality:** Look at the bond's underlying rating to determine the relative risk compared to similar bonds.
3. **Debt coverage:** Does the debt coverage leave sufficient margin of error for unanticipated future problems?
4. **Issue size:** Is there sufficient liquidity to support a market that will allow you to get out if necessary?
5. **Maturity distribution:** Where is the bond in the company's maturity distribution? How much debt must be paid to others before it gets to you?
6. **TRACE history:** Look up the bond on TRACE to see where it has been trading and the liquidity the bond has.

7. **Yield:** Does the yield you are offered justify the risk you are taking? If yes, then find out the spread over a comparable maturing bond on the U.S. Treasury curve to determine what your yield should be. See if they match. If they do, then pull the trigger. If they don't, then negotiate the price until they do. If you can't get the right price, then walk away.

8. **Fair price:** Is the price you're willing to pay to get the yield you need close to the market? If not, then you'll have to negotiate with your brokers and be prepared to walk away if they can't meet you in between.

Checklist for Municipal Bonds

The pre-order checklist for municipal bonds has many of the same headings as does the checklist for corporates. However, the questions are sometimes a bit different. Here's the municipal bond checklist:

Municipal Bond Checklist

1. **Diversification:** Does the nature of this bond (revenue, general obligation, or something else) along with issuer's geographic location help diversify your bond portfolio?

2. **Credit quality:** Look at the bond's underlying rating without any bond insurance to determine the relative risk compared to similar bonds. There are just three bond insurance companies with the financial resources to rely on their bond insurance policies: Assured Guaranty Corp, Berkshire Hathaway Assurance, and Financial Security Assurance, Inc. Any other insurance is suspect and not reliable.

3. **Repayment sources:** Consider the likelihood that the issuer's repayment sources will remain intact. For general obligations bonds (GOs) and many double-barreled bonds, this is not a problem. For certain revenue issues, it can be.

4. **Issue size:** Is there sufficient liquidity to support a market that will allow you to get out if necessary?

5. **Maturity distribution:** Where is the bond in the municipality's maturity distribution? Will it be able to pay you before it runs out of money?

6. **TRACE history:** Look up the bond on TRACE to see where it has been trading and the liquidity the bond has. This will also tell you the prices of the most recent trades.

7. **Fair price:** Is the price you're willing to pay to get the yield you need close to the market? If not, then you'll have to negotiate with your brokers and be prepared to walk away if they can't meet you in between.

8. **Yield:** Municipal bonds should have less risk than corporates. The yield you are offered should reflect that. Still, you should find out the spread to a comparable maturing bond on the U.S. Treasury curve to determine what your yield should be. If they match, then you're getting a fair price. If they don't, then negotiate with your broker. Be prepared to walk away if you can't get a fair price rather than overpay.

Armed with your understanding of bond execution, we're now ready to dive into some of the bond market's problems. Chapter 5, Don't Repeat What Has Gone Wrong, shows by example the pitfalls of so many bond investors and how to avoid them.

CHAPTER 5

Learning from Mistakes

The only safe way to double your money is to fold it over once and put it in your pocket.

Words to live by. You've probably heard that before, especially during troubled economic times. There is a way to protect your portfolio and keep it working hard for you so that there is never any question regarding the safety of your money.

Every investor learns the most not from his successes but from his mistakes. Chapter 5 takes us through the odyssey of a fictitious investor (we call *El Greedo*) before the 2008 credit crisis hit. The asset allocations and concentrated risk you'll see in *El Greedo's* portfolio are too often the rule rather than the exception for individual investors. We've seen it time and time again. We begin with *El Greedo's* portfolio before the 2008 credit crisis hit.

Portfolio Composition: Pre-credit Crisis

Take a look at *El Greedo's* bond portfolio (see Table 5.1). What does it tell you about the man?

Keep in mind that you are looking at his dismal performance with 20/20 hindsight. The fault is not entirely his own. *El Greedo* is a smart man. A little headstrong, perhaps, but definitely not dumb. He made his money in the used auto parts business. Unfortunately, he ran his bond portfolio the same way he ran his company—his

Table 5.1 *El Greedo's* Portfolio

Pre-2008 Credit Crisis	
Security Description	Composition %
HRPT PPTYS TR NT Income Notes 6.5% Due 01-15-13	5%
Fund American Cos 5.875% Due 05-15-13	6%
American Express 7.3% Due 08-20-13	6%
American General Financial Income Notes 6% Due 12-15-14	6%
Hartford Life Insurance Income Notes 6% Due 06-15-16	5%
General Electric 5.4% Due 02-15-17	8%
Citigroup Inc Notes 5.5% Due 02-15-17	8%
JP Morgan Chase & Co 6.125% Due 06-27-17	8%
General Motors Accep Smart Notes 7.25% Due 09-15-17	5%
Wells Fargo Co 5.625% Due 12-11-17	8%
Dell Inc 5.650% Due 04-15-18	4%
General Motors Accep Smart Notes 6.35% Due 04-15-19	9%
Donnelley RR & Sons 8.875% Due 04-15-21	6%
GE Capital Internotes 5.8% Due 11-15-23	8%
General Motors Accep 8% Due 11-01-31	8%
	100%

way or the highway. He never asked for anyone's opinions and rarely took advice. Greedoz Partz, Inc., flourished nonetheless. So did his bonds, for a while.

Then his stubborn ways caught up with him. You can see the overconcentration in financials that he owned. They provided a nice return. But when the crisis of 2008 made landfall, he gave it all back plus a huge chunk of his principal. Such an undue concentration in a single industry is like sitting at the roulette wheel and putting a huge bet on a single number. If it comes up, then you're rich. If not, you've lost your wad. Odds are that you'll lose.

El Greedo thought he was diversifying out of financials when he bought the IncomeNotes and the SmartNotes. He apparently didn't realize that the SmartNotes issued by GMAC, General Motors Acceptance Corp., were actually from a financial company. The IncomeNotes were issued by insurance giant, AIG, yet another financial company. To add insult to injury, these were very small retail issues with no liquidity. *El Greedo* couldn't get out of them even if he had tried, which he didn't.

El Greedo was a yield junkie—someone who values yield above all else. Above safety. Above liquidity. Above diversification. Note that every position in his portfolio was there to do one thing: Produce yield. The companies with which *El Greedo* populated his corporate bond portfolio threw off all sorts of yield. Why? There's a rate for every risk. The financials were the largest issuers. They had to entice investors with juicier yields to get them to buy the bonds.

This single-focus mindset illustrates how *El Greedo* failed to build a group of bonds with specific jobs to do. A more balanced portfolio might have one industry group provide counter-cyclical stability. Another might be there to exploit potential in a rising industry. Yet another has the job of providing stable income without regard to economic fluctuations. Instead, *El Greedo* put all of his eggs in a single basket. He got scrambled during the 2008 credit crisis.

Another problem with *El Greedo's* single asset approach is that he relied on what the company's management and the analysts told him. These people don't have investors' best interests at heart. Their agenda was something entirely different. Further, as we found out, these people often don't have the facts right themselves.

The Credit Crisis Hits

Among the first to feel the punch of 2008's credit crisis were *Greedo's* beloved financials. Their quarterly write-downs of losses routinely exceeded the amount reserved. Right there, *Greedo* should have seen a problem with management's grasp of their business.

The handwriting was on the wall. All *Greedo* had to do was read the financial headlines. GE Capital, Citigroup, and Goldman Sachs all had trouble raising the capital needed to keep them afloat. Indeed, the venerable Goldman Sachs turned to Warren Buffett as their lender of last resort. Still *Greedo* didn't change his bond strategy and hung onto his financials for dear life.

"Just a temporary hiccup," he said. "They'll come back. You'll see. These companies are too big to fail. They have to make it." He confided only in himself, "I'm in too deep to take such losses."

Fail? Now *El Greedo* is using the F-word? Sounds like he's enjoying the introspective moment all investors have just before they capitulate and admit they were wrong.

There is a reason for *Greedo's* obstinacy. He had no choice but to believe these problems would work themselves out. He invested with his ego rather than his brain. He lulled himself into wrongly believing prices would quickly come back and prove him smart once again.

Sound even vaguely familiar? Do you know an investor with some (or all) of *El Greedo's* predilections? There's no shame in admitting it. The only shame for such investors is in stubbornly refusing to rebalance their portfolio. Instead, they sit there watching their losses pile up.

El Greedo was oblivious to the big picture unfolding before his eyes: The entire U.S. economy was crumbling. By the time he realized it, it was too late. This guaranteed his portfolio problems would worsen. *Greedo's* mistake was that he failed to change strategies when the market told him to.

Results: Portfolio Annihilation

Greedo had one obvious problem that caused his demise: He relied almost exclusively—85 percent of the total portfolio—on the financial sector. Yes, there were a number of names represented. Some even had the names of other industries within their names. However, at the end of the day, they were all either financials or heavily financial related.

General Electric Was One

We discovered earlier that GE is just a hedge fund in drag, owing its profits to the GE Capital division. GE embarked on a series of capital raises. Like a bouncing ball losing momentum, with each raise, the bonds' bounce off their lows became smaller and smaller. Why? Because the news continued to get worse as management was forced to disclose more of GE Capital's over-leveraged balance sheet.

The company needed continued access to the capital markets to continue feeding its voracious appetite for money. Yet, management was not forthcoming in describing GE's problems. When this lack of disclosure was made public by the financial press, it worsened GE's credit problems. At the height of arrogance, GE management must have thought public transparency was something other companies had to do. They were forced to take TARP money.

GMAC Was Another

GMAC was formerly known as General Motors Acceptance Corporation. It isn't a car manufacturer. Oh no. The word *acceptance* in its old name refers to financial paper—just another financial industry participant. The company was created by General Motors to be its financing arm. Then, in 2006 GM sold 51 percent to a consortium headed by Cerberus Capital. Cerberus also owned Chrysler before its bankruptcy. GMAC's residential housing unit, ResCap, had been rocked by the housing downturn. It was the country's second largest mortgage lender behind Countrywide Financial. During 2007 GMAC lost a whopping $2.3 billion due to ResCap's huge loss of $4.4 billion.

Bank of America Didn't Help El Greedo Either

Although BOA did somewhat better than the others, its management failed to understand the tremendous problems acquisition of Merrill Lynch created. The Merrill problems stemmed from derivatives, collateralized debt obligations, collateralized mortgage obligations, credit default swaps, and sub-prime mortgages. All the toxic junk that almost brought down the U.S. banking system was moldering on Boa's balance sheet. Worse still, Merrill's corporate ego required it to do everything in huge size. All these toxic securities Merrill had on its balance sheet, it had in spades

Worse still, Chairman John Thain, never understood Merrill's problems. It seems that BOA's entire executive suite and its risk management team were asleep at the switch. They were forced to take TARP money along with the others.

Goldie Didn't Help Either

Goldman Sachs, the financial market's perpetual Golden Gloves champ, found itself sinking with all the others. Goldie was shut out from the capital markets for the first time. Capital is the lifeblood of the financial industry. Without it, profit margins shrink to nothing, earnings decline, and so do stock and bond prices. Goldman finally turned to Warren Buffett for a loan.

What *El Greedo* hadn't anticipated was that a global financial crisis sinks all ships. Goldman Sachs was tarred with the same brush as the others. Some say wrongly because it didn't have the exposure to as many toxic assets as the others. In the end, it too was forced to take TARP money.

Down for the Count

The momentum of the downturn carried the dwindling value of *El Greedo's* portfolio over the falls. The U.S.' economic mess didn't happen overnight, nor did it occur behind closed doors. The information was available in the financial press just for the taking. *Greedo* just couldn't bear to hear it. He was too shell-shocked to take action as he watched his losses mount daily. The professionals (who lost big too) would say that *El Greedo* simply didn't stick to a valid trading discipline. That's true. Instead, he structured a hugely risky bond portfolio that was trying to swing for the fences. This highly speculative strategy turned against him.

El Greedo's *Downsized Portfolio Value*

It wasn't pretty. The value of *Greedo's* portfolio dropped a good 30 percent in just six months. The fact that he wasn't alone and that indeed most of the industry's top professionals suffered the same fate was small consolation. *Greedo* thought he was smarter than the market. Nobody is.

He was up against a wall. Unless *Greedo* did something and quickly, he would have to change his retirement lifestyle. He had wanted to enjoy his wealth generated from the sale of Greedoz Partz. He saw himself taking lavish vacations. Kiss that goodbye. He anticipated getting a new, flashy car every few years. Not anymore. What worried him the most, though, was how to tell his grandkids—whom he put into fancy private schools and promised to pay for tuition—that they would soon have to enroll in public school.

El Greedo has now lost whatever margin of error there once was in his investment accounts. More to his plight, there's no more time to ride the portfolio down, hoping it'll come back. Maybe it will; maybe it won't. *Greedo* can't afford to find out. Not if he wants any hope of living the retirement lifestyle he thought he would.

Emergency Financial Surgery

El finally got religion. He realized that he needed to do something drastic. We call this rebalancing the portfolio in the post-credit crisis environment. There's no shame in doing such financial surgery on a bond portfolio. It is healthy and necessary, especially when changes occur in the market environment. The shame would have been if *El* continued on his earlier path.

But he didn't. Instead, he built a fortress of safety around his portfolio. He applied the same good common business sense to his investment accounts that had made Greedoz Partz successful. Here are the changes that *El* made to his bond portfolio.

Diversify Out of a Single Industry

El learned that the financials weren't his friend. The greater lesson that he finally took to heart was that his choice of the financials was just a symptom of a larger problem. He had become a one-trick pony—learning just one investment category and attempting to exploit it. That's not investing. It is raw speculation.

El's first step toward redemption and financial recovery was painful. He sold mostly all of the positions in his original portfolio. These were at a loss from where he bought them. The day of reckoning came when his losses went from unrealized—just paper losses—to realized losses. It was a humbling and bitter pill to swallow. Especially for a man who was his own boss for so many years and exited at the top of a very tough, competitive industry. Still, he cowboyed up and did what was necessary. To his credit, *El* didn't waste a minute pouting or second guessing himself. He moved on with his diversification strategy.

El doubled the names in his portfolio from the original 14 on his list to 29. These additional companies allowed him to expand the representation even within industry categories—a wise thing to do when building an investment fortress.

He studied the various industry groups. He selected a diversified representation of those companies he expected would fulfill his new goals of safety, liquidity, and yield. Some he chose for their growth potential—such as tech and conglomerates. After all, *El* still fancied himself somewhat a player, although he had managed to rein in this character flaw. He also added some industries for their reliable income stream—railroads, telecom, scientific and healthcare manufacturers. For others—waste disposal and transportation—he deliberately accepted a lower yield in order to get the safety and liquidity they offered.

Table 5.2   Rebalanced Portfolio Concentration

Rebalanced Industry Concentrations	
Waste	3%
Manufacturing	19%
Telecom	7%
Service	10%
Cable	3%
Financials	12%
Pharmaceuticals	8%
Utilities	6%
Energy	17%
Retail	8%
Tobacco	4%
Food	3%
	100%

When he was done rebalancing his industry categories, *El* was satisfied that some would be counter-cyclical to others. For example, when retailers like Best Buy went down, telecoms like BellSouth would be up, countering the hit in value to the overall portfolio. These industry choices served as the cornerstones of *Fortress Greedo*. Overall, the industries he selected for his newly rebalanced portfolio are shown in Table 5.2.

As seen in Table 5.2, his three largest industry categories were weighted in favor of manufacturing, energy and financials. However, that concentration isn't as bad as it sounds. *El's* manufacturing companies were in a variety of different sectors including healthcare equipment (Quest Diagnostics), fiber optics and tech-related glass products (Corning), computers (Dell), and electronic components (Tyco), along with some others. The companies he selected in energy included oil exploration and production (Pacific Energy Partners), midstream services and interstate transport and storage of energy products (Energy Transfer Partners), a refiner (Premcor), and drilling equipment provider, Weatherford International.

Still somewhat in love with the financials, *El* was careful to diversify within that sector. He chose a money transfer company (Western Union), a company that leases capital assets (GATX Corp.), and

Jefferies, the investment banking firm. *El* finally learned not to load up the boat with banks that are all subject to the same risks.

El also promised himself not to allocate more than 3 to 5 percent of the total portfolio to any one name. He succeeded, rising up to the 5 percent maximum just once with Staples bonds.

Results of the Rebalance

Some of *El's* bonds will be either called or mature. He'll replace them with like bonds relative to the category's risk and liquidity characteristics. The point is that he built himself a well-diversified and totally rebalanced portfolio from the loser he had before. Now he is ensured limited downside and has a predictable income stream that is safe from assaults on the fortress.

Of course things can and will go wrong. *El* can guess where and when it will happen. At the end of the day, it is only a guess. However, when it happens, he has only experienced a minor loss compared to the devastation suffered by *El Greedo's* original portfolio.

 Action Step: Turn Pain Into Gain

When rebalancing your portfolio, take the pain to get the gain. Take the loss and buy the right bonds needed to rebalance the portfolio.

Properly Rebalanced Portfolio

El worked diligently on his rebalanced portfolio. He studied the industries in which he was interested. He got a feel for what role he thought each would play as the U.S. economy climbs out of its second worst economic disaster in history.

For better or for worse, *El* believed that consumer electronics—especially home theater systems—was one sector that would become a favorite as families opt for stay-at-home evenings rather than going out. He selected such names as Royal Phillips, Sony, LG Electronics, Samsung, Corning, and Panasonic to research. He looked up reports on their bonds that the credit analysts had prepared. He selected a couple of his favorites to begin tracking their bond prices on TRACE. With a feel for the market and what the right price should be, he began speaking with his *three* favorite brokers—all of whom he had accounts with. When a broker was able to meet his price, he purchased the Corning bonds.

Sound painstaking? You bet. Especially when you consider that *El* followed this structured procedure for each of the 29 names on his rebalancing list. With his industry categories selected, he set to work on populating them with bonds from the corporations he thought would contribute the most toward achieving his goals of safety, liquidity, and yield. It took him three months to populate his newly rebalanced portfolio the way he wanted it. Table 5.3 shows the bonds and their respective allocations within the entire portfolio.

Is He Done?

No. In fact, *El* has only just begun managing his bond portfolio like an investor rather than a novice speculator destined to blow up his wealth. Each day or so he spends some quality time reviewing what is happening to the companies whose bonds he owns as well as the industries in which they compete. He monitors the overall portfolio's performance. He wants to be sure that his assumptions about which bonds are up when their opposites are down remain correct.

He tracks his company's ratings by Moody's and Standard & Poor's. Any hint of future change gets his immediate attention. If a bond appears ready for downgrade, *El* immediately checks his own risk criteria associated with the bond itself, not just with the rating agencies. If the bond now falls outside his risk tolerance, he sells it. The rating agencies are more of a warning system, rather than the definitive authority they once were. And he's always on the lookout for new ideas in Bondland coming from the business magazines, the broadcast media, as well as the two newsletters to which he subscribes. *El* is now an educated man in the world of corporate bonds.

Is He Up or Is He Down?

Both. Immediately after selling his lopsided portfolio, then rebalancing it using an investor's strategy, he was down. Of course he was. After all, *El Greedo* had to convert what, until the time of sale, were only unrecognized losses to recognized—real-world, big-boy—losses. From that standpoint, his portfolio was down over $1 million from his original investment value.

Table 5.3 Properly Balanced Portfolio

Post-2008 Credit Crisis

Security Description	% Composition
ALLIED WASTE NORTH AMER INC SR 5.75% Due 02-15-11	3%
QUEST DIAGNOSTICS INC SRNT 7.5% Due 07-12-11	3%
TELECOM ITALIA CAP GTD SRNT 6.2% Due 07-18-11	3%
XEROX CORP SRNTS 6.875% Due 08-15-11	3%
TIME WARNER INC 5.5% Due 11-15-11	3%
WESTERN UN CO NT 5.4% Due 11-17-11	4%
AMERISOURCEBERGEN CORP SRNT 5.625% Due 09-15-12	4%
FISERV INC SRNT 6.125% Due 11-20-12	4%
GENENTECH INC SRNT 4.75% Due 07-01-13	4%
NATIONAL RURAL UTILS COOP FIN 5.5% Due 07-01-13	4%
ENERGY TRANSFER PART NOTES CAL 6% Due 07-01-13	3%
BEST BUY INC NT 6.75% Due 07-15-13	3%
PACKAGING CORP AMER 3RNT 5.75% Due 08-01-13	3%
ALTRIA GROUP INC 8.5% Due 11-10-13	4%
FEDEX CORP NOTE 7.375% Due 01-15-14	3%
STAPLES INC NOTE 9.75% Due 01-15-14	5%
CONAGRA FOODS INC NOTES 5.875% Due 04-15-14	3%
GATX CORP NOTES 8.75% Due 05-15-14	4%
BELLSOUTH CORP BONDS 5.2% Due 09-15-14	4%
ENTERPRISE PRODS OPERLP 5% Due 03-01-15	4%
CORNING INC 6.05% Due 06-15-15	3%
FISHER SCIENTIFIC INTLINC 3R3B 6.125% Due 07-01-15	3%
PREMCOR REFNG GROUP INC 7.5% Due 06-15-15	3%
PACIFIC ENERGY PARTNERSL P SRN 6.25% Due 09-15-15	3%
JEFFERIES GROUP 5.50% Due 3-15-16	4%
CENTERPOINT ENERGY RES CORP 6.15% Due 05-01-16	2%
WEATHERFORD INTL INC GTDSRNT 6.35% Due 06-15-17	4%
DELL INC NT 5.65% Due 04-15-18	4%
TYCO INTL GROUP S A GTDNT PUT 8.5% Due 01-15-19	3%
	100%

However, he will be well ahead of the game going forward. Fortress Greedo is well built and strong. He positioned it to withstand most assaults he could think of.

- Capricious politicians seeking to curry favor with voting union members at enormous cost to the bondholders.

- Economic calamity resulting from financial instruments of dubious merit engineered by greedy Wall Streeters solely for the purpose of earning a commission.
- Geographic catastrophe.
- Off-shore competition from those to whom the United States taught the business and are now cleaning our clock competitively.

El estimates that his corporate bond portfolio will be able to withstand the stresses and strains of whatever the financial markets throw at it. Certainly, much better than his old, overly concentrated portfolio and his speculative way of doing things that almost cost him his retirement. Further, he now has a steady income stream that is not dependent on a single industry and just a few companies within it. Nor are his fortunes subject to the whims of a handful of ego-driven CEO's catering to regulators, governmental czars overseeing their industry, and stockholders without regard to their creditors. Chapter 6, Egos Gone Wild, lays bare the excesses of these few and shows how quickly their mistakes can decimate a bond portfolio.

CHAPTER 6

Egos Gone Wild

Bondholders have a much longer term stake in the company than do its stock holders—especially those traders who are in and out of the stock. Bondholders are wedded to the management team for five years, 10 years, and often much longer. So management's judgment, stability, and overall concern for the company's balance sheet are crucial to bondholders. We don't want to lend our money to a CEO whose ego has gone wildly off the deep end.

Chapter 6, Egos Gone Wild, uses some of the more notorious managers as examples of what to look for in an unstable executive suite that is driven not by the responsibility borne from being an investor fiduciary but instead by personal greed. By the end of this chapter you will be able to identify an ego-driven management team. You'll know what to do when a once well-run company turns over its management team and replaces competence with something that is not friendly to debt holders.

Succession Is a Lost Art

There once was a time when the captains of industry who ran blue chip companies were paid in parallel with the return they provided their shareholders. The companies were legendary for their stability and management expertise: General Electric, American Express, General Motors, Chrysler Corp., Goldman Sachs, Citicorp (before it was Citigroup), Merrill Lynch, and AIG. Today these same names carry the taint of incompetence, disgrace, and bankruptcy. Their C-suite executives were asleep at the controls. They lost sight of the investors' interests and replaced them with their own personal agenda. Management's compensation somehow became decoupled from performance.

What happened? The extraordinarily capable CEO's failed at their final critical task: Find an equally competent successor. It took extraordinary individuals to build large, complex companies. They had debt, sure. But it was manageable. The balance sheet worked for bondholders. The CEOs knew that if investors suffered due to a lack of performance, so would their paychecks.

Those chosen to take their places hadn't built the companies they were hired to run. They were handed the reins and told to do the best they could. They stepped into a complicated quagmire that made sense only to the architect. The builder was the only one who knew how the puzzle fit together and where all the bodies were buried. This person succeeded in coupling power and authority with deep personal relationships among the very people who worked with them in the trenches to build the company to what it was. And now this person was gone.

Successors were viewed with skepticism and distrust. After all, they had some very big shoes to fill. When Vikram Pandit took over Citigroup from Charlie Prince in December 2008, he had to understand how this huge colossus all fit together. The first thing he did to get his feet under him was embark on a world tour of Citi's offices. Pandit's world tour took him to the farthest reaches of the realm he inherited—Asia, Europe, the Middle East, even South Korea and Poland.

Too many successor CEOs stumble shortly after landing in the pilot's seat. It seems there's a thread of commonality that bond-holders must look for when there's a change of control. Watch the financial press for these eight traits in the new boss:

1. He appears to be in over his head.
2. He has little or no experience at the top job in a similar company. Indeed, watch for quotes like, "Management is management. You master the principles and you can run any kind of company." This is absurd when applied to the multinational financial conglomerates employing hundreds of thousands of workers.
3. Despite what the board's compensation committee says, watch for the CEO's pay package being decoupled from shareholder value and balance sheet stability. Especially look for stock

buy-back programs, stock option repricing, and reset features related to the CEO's pay package.

4. Look for a board of directors that is still the Chairman's personal group of rubber stampers. Find out by looking in the corporate governance section of the company web site and read the director selection committee's charter to determine how the directors arrive at the board table.

5. The new CEO takes too long and ultimately fails to understand the company, its dynamics in the marketplace, and its risk assessment. This failure makes it seem to the financial community that we are all being lied to by the CEO. Sometimes it's intentional; often it's just out of ignorance of the situation and a failure to understand the company.

6. The new CEO is way too slow to understand and act on market indicators signaling a downturn.

7. Denial of the extent of the company's problems. Watch for statements in the press that are unsubstantiated, unsupported, or just plain silly when compared with common sense.

8. A corporate culture of fear where subordinate managers are afraid to blow the whistle for fear they will lose their place at the corporate trough.

CEO Compensation: The Great Disconnect

Bondholders demand a direct link between CEO compensation and corporate performance. As the company's creditors, we want to see accountability and financial incentive for maintaining the means to service our debt. If there's a disconnect in this vital linkage, at some time (maybe not this year or even next) the company will sink and with it, the value of our bonds. Since we hold such long-term positions in corporate bonds, we look for hiccups in compensation policy that could have far-reaching impacts.

Sometimes history has shown a company's stock rising despite the antics of its CEO. This most often occurs in a general equity bull market, which tends to float all boats, even those with holes in them. An example of this false positive is Citigroup. The bull market of the post-tech wreck masked titanic flaws in Citi's overall business model. Only when the market suddenly turned downward did the full horror of its management decisions surface. This created catastrophic consequences to Citi's bondholders.

How did this affect CEO, Vikram Pandit? He earned $38 million in 2008 (third highest paid financial CEO) as the company lost $27.7 billion and remained afloat only by the U.S. taxpayers coughing up another $45 billion in bailout money. To be fair, Pandit cut his salary the next year to just $1, saying that he gets the new reality.

The second place finisher in the 2008 compensation derby was Ken Chenault of American Express. He carted away almost $43 million in salary and stock awards. Chenault has the dubious distinction of topping Bloomberg's ranking of financial CEOs who provided the *least* value for the money they earned. Under his very expensive watch, Amex's stock return was down 69 percent from the previous year.

Decision Point

The decision that bondholders must make is described simply. Actually following through is another case entirely. Here's the decision: If we own bonds issued by a company whose CEO is hugely rewarded for his own failure, then executive pay is disconnected from performance. There is no incentive for him to keep the corporate ship of state afloat. There is no culture of shareholder stewardship. Instead, the corporate culture is one of anything goes, just so I get what's mine. It flows like brown sludge from the C-suite, down the hall to the boardroom and all the way out to the mail room. It is only a matter of time before the company implodes from this cancer and bond debt service stops. Sell the bonds while you can.

 Action Step: CEO Pay Must Result from Performance

If the CEO's compensation is unrelated to the company's performance, they do not own that company's bonds. If they are now in your portfolio, sell them. If you were considering buying them, don't.

Watch for Stock Buy-Backs

Bondholders are constantly looking for the canary in the coal mine. All we ask for is a simple, early warning system of trouble. One of the best alarms we've found is a company's share repurchase program.

Such programs foretell where the CEO's interests truly lie—especially if he's using borrowed funds to pay for the stock buy-back. The purpose of such programs is to raise the stock price. Why incur debt for no business purpose other than to give a pop to the stockholders? The answer below shouldn't surprise you. Understand that these stock price increases are often temporary. However, the debt incurred isn't. It will last for years.

Every dollar of new debt incurred weakens the company's ability to service existing debt. There's only so much debt a company can sustain before the capital markets turn off the spigot. Bondholders ask why management would cash in those precious chips just to raise the stock price.

The answer illustrates the CEOs' orientation. Often they are under pressure by the institutional investors, stock promoters, and other stakeholders who want to dump the stock when it reaches a high water mark.

Then there are the executives and board members whose stock options are due to expire. They want to get the stock up as high as possible before expiration to increase their profit—often in the tens of millions. Additionally, the higher the stock when these options are exercised, the less price dilution to existing equity shareholders. This can mask what is actually happening.

If they sell at the right time, the shareholders who ride up the stock price resulting from such buy-back programs actually do win. But they're the only ones. The company has incurred a huge debt—often in the hundreds of millions or billions. The employees haven't benefited. The bondholders are left holding the bag. They did not get any benefit and must deal with the additional burden the new debt places on the company's balance sheet.

Stock buy-back programs using borrowed funds are unfriendly to the bondholders' interests. If you own bonds in such a company, look closely at what the bond analysts say about it. The stress tests may reveal a reduced margin of error. It may seem likely the market for this company's products will decline. If you see these things on the horizon, then sell the bonds while you can still get a bid.

Games with Stock Option Pricing

A sure way to tell if a CEO's compensation is unlinked with his performance is when the board reprices the CEO's stock options.

This most often occurs when the CEO's performance is so dismal that the stock price falls so far below his options strike price that they're valueless. The CEO convinces the board that the fall in the stock price is not his fault. He asks them to reprice his options at a lower price so that he can make some real money before they expire. This is how faltering CEOs and directors have made hundreds of millions while their companies are falling off a cliff. By granting this request, the board rewards the CEO for failure. It has decoupled his compensation from the company's performance.

 Action Step: Don't Loan to Companies Who Reprice Stock Options

If you own the bonds of a company that makes a habit of repricing executive stock options—that is, rewards failure—then sell the bonds.

Watch for Ego Problems

CEOs of public companies certainly have egos. That's healthy. It takes a dynamic individual to tell so many employees, investors, the financial media, and those on Wall Street who watch his every move, "Follow Me. I know the way." The problem comes when that ego gets out of control. The CEO begins making decisions less for the good of the company and its stakeholders and more to prop up his own agenda. Sometimes that agenda begins and ends with ME.

How do bondholders tell if a company has a CEO whose ego has gone wild? These are six telltale symptoms:

1. **Watch the news:** Look for high salaries and stock options and how both are linked to performance. Is the CEO reported as behaving oddly in public, such as at press conferences or shareholder meetings? Has there been a lifestyle change such as a divorce and immediate remarriage to a bimbo 30 years his junior?
2. **Monuments:** Companies can sometimes take on the persona of their ego-driven CEOs. Naming public monuments and events after the company becomes the same to the ego-driven CEO

as seeing his own name up there. Sports stadiums are famous: Wrigley Field is now U.S. Cellular Field; the San Francisco Giants now play at SBC Park; the Lakers play at Staples Center. The list goes on. PGA golf events are no different: The Mercedes Benz Championship, The Honda Classic, The Shell Houston Open. Studies show that shortly after naming the monument the company hits the skids.

3. **Cash balances and uses:** Does the company use its cash for machinery and equipment—disbursements that help the company make money? Is it buying back debt to improve the balance sheet? This is a bond-friendly move. Or, is it buying back its own stock to make the CEO appear a hero to investors?

4. **Stable management:** Look for a game of musical chairs in the executive suite. Such management instability is not in the bondholders' interest.

5. **Successor's background:** Many aging CEOs have named an heir apparent. Their backgrounds are usually published. Study them. Ask yourself if you would hire this guy to run the company that owes you money. More on this later.

6. **Acquisitions financing:** Statistics show that 80 percent of most acquisitions fail to accomplish their goals—industry consolidation, cost reduction, entry into new market, etc. Acquisitions are a crap shoot. Ask how the company finances its acquisitions. Is it stock? Or, contrary to bondholder's interests, is it with cash or debt?

The Case of Citigroup

Sandy Weil was acquisition-minded. His Travelers Group included the brokerage Smith Barney, and he had just a year earlier bought Salomon Brothers for $9 billion. Now he had insurance, securities brokerage, and investment banking. His ambition was to create a world-wide, one-stop supermarket for all things financial. He got his opportunity in 1998 with the $37.4 billion merger of his Travelers Group with John Reed's Citicorp.

The colossus Weil created had too many disparate business units. It was impossible to integrate them all so the company could capitalize on the synergy Weil expected. However, the roaring bull market saved him. Citigroup stock was on a terror despite the disconnect between its business units and the financial engineering the company used to make its profits. As a result, Weil's business model was never tested while he was in power.

Weil hand-picked his successor, Chuck Prince, as CEO in 2003. Turns out Weil didn't choose very carefully. Prince was a lawyer by trade. He worked in the general counsel's office of U.S. Steel for a time. Then moved on to Commercial Credit Company in various capacities. He joined Citi sometime after 1995 and ran its global investment banking group. He became CEO then was elected to Citi's board in 2006. He consolidated his power quickly by becoming a member of its Compensation Committee and Chairman of its Nominating and Corporate Governance Committee. Now he had a say in how much everyone was paid and who got to make the big decisions.

Prince was fired in November 2007 after Citi reported huge and unexpected losses on the order of $14 billion, largely the result of the Bank's investment in sub-prime mortgages. Still, Prince managed to walk away with a shopping cart full of salary, perks, and stock worth just under $100 million. There was a significant disconnect between performance and pay.

It turns out that Citi was not only involved in sub-prime mortgages. Under Prince, it developed a taste for everything toxic, including the infamous collateralized debt obligations and credit default swaps. They used off balance sheet special purpose entities to create sufficient leverage to load up the boat with these toxic assets. It proved their undoing.

When Citi's fortress began crumbling, Prince had little clue how to assess the damage and stop the capital from bleeding out. Bad news for bondholders. Investors publicly cried for Prince's ouster. He was replaced by Vikram Pandit in 2008. At the time of this writing, rumors are that Citi's new owner, the U.S. government, is considering replacing Pandit.

Figure 6.1 shows how Citi's stock peaked shortly before Prince was named. It was downhill from there. Still, the board thanked Prince by allowing him to walk away with a king's ransom.

Much the same thing happened at Merrill Lynch. Chairman David Komansky hand selected Stanley O'Neil as his successor in 2003. Again, it appeared that O'Neil had little idea of the tremendous risk his company was taking in the financial derivatives markets. He allowed Merrill's balance sheet to turn into a toxic cesspool. Eventually, Merrill wrote off something close to $30 billion. For that

Figure 6.1   Citigroup Stock Chart

Source: Bloomberg Finance L.P. © 2009 Bloomberg Finance L.P. All rights reserved. Used with permission.

dismal performance, O'Neil received a severance package worth an astounding $157 million.

Merrill's board wasn't yet finished reducing the company's value. In O'Neil's place, they hired John Thain. Certainly, Thain inherited a mess. The economy's plunge didn't help matters. Still, in early 2008 Thain told the financial press at an investor conference in New York, "Our core franchise is very strong . . . we're actually quite optimistic." Then, of course, who could forget the $2 million remodeling of his personal office at shareholder expense? Items that seemed to highlight his departure from the reality of Merrill's dire circumstances included:

- Area rug valued at $87,000
- Nineteenth-century credenza priced at $68,000
- Two guest chairs at $88,000
- George IV chair discounted to $18,000

- Commode on legs at $35,000
- Thain's personal chauffeur cost the company $230,000 for his one year of work

These are expenses that royalty would normally incur, not the CEO of a publicly traded company whose stakeholders watch the value of their investment plummet to new lows seemingly every day. Bank of America (Merrill's new owner) CEO, Ken Lewis canned Thain (see Figure 6.2).

Not only was Thain's $43 million salary disconnected from performance, he brought a new and very public arrogance to the table. The fancy office and his apparent sense of entitlement without earning it enraged stock- and bondholders.

There are two women who also fall into the category of huge pay for royal screw-ups. Jill Barad, former CEO of Mattel, left with a severance package worth $50 million. The compensation committee paid

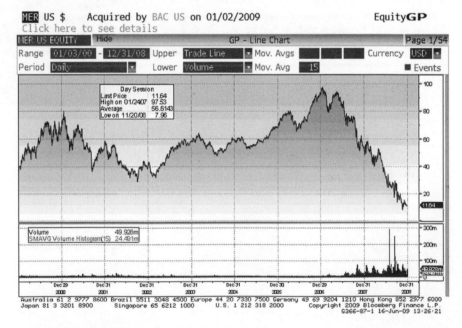

Figure 6.2   Merrill Stock Chart

Source: Bloomberg Finance L.P. © 2009 Bloomberg Finance L.P. All rights reserved. Used with permission.

her $26 million in severance, then gave her a $5 million life insurance policy for life and her office furniture (probably not in the league of John Thain's but very nice, nonetheless). They also forgave her home loan from the company and paid the resulting income taxes for her. All this, in exchange for a vast series of underperforming financial results.

Don't forget Hewlett-Packard's former Chair, Carly Fiorina. After plunging the company's value, she waltzed out the door with $14 million in severance. This was the company's standard package: 2.5 times her salary plus her targeted bonus. Forget the fact that there was no way she would have earned that targeted bonus based on the company's results on her watch. The board also allowed her to exercise 6.1 million *unvested* stock options one year past her termination.

The Take-Away

There's a pattern in the disconnect between executive pay and the company's results. When companies fail to demand performance from their executives and still bestow on them huge pay packages, bondholders will suffer. The balance sheet will either crumble from short-term remedies such as debt-financed stock buy-back programs or it will crumble from sheer incompetence. But it will crumble.

Watch for the inflated ego of the CEO who created the company in the first place. Nobody can do as good a job as him, and he's going to prove it by naming incompetent, unqualified people to succeed him. Sandy Weil did it when he selected Charlie Prince. Jack Welch, Chairman of General Electric, did it when he chose Jeff Imelt as his successor.

We haven't spent much time on the crooks. Bondholders are unlikely to forget Bernie Ebbers, Chairman of WorldCom, and Kenneth Lay, the now deceased Chairman of Enron. Both shared something in common with the others: They were arrogant with the public and created a culture of *what's in it for me*. All when they were supposed to be stewards of the investor's interests.

Their egos and unbridled greed got in the way of their fiduciary duties to the stakeholders. Instead, they placed their own interests ahead of the investors and bondholders. They took their eye off the ball and their hands off the wheel. Instead they focused exclusively on their own wallets.

A New Trend . . . Again

Some may see an emerging bright spot for bond investors even though the financial companies have hit the press with so many horror stories. There's a trend of de-leveraging. This is just a fancy way of saying some companies—Ford, Dow Chemical, and Hertz are three—have issued stock and used the proceeds in part to call in some of their bonds. Yes, some would think this is very bond-friendly.

Indeed, according to Bloomberg News, 165 companies raised $87 billion in equity sales during the first quarter of 2009. About 77 percent of those companies used at least some of the money to slash their debt. This de-leveraging and balance sheet repair is not quite as altruistic as it may seem. When faced with the possibility of defaulting on their bonds, what CEO wouldn't first dilute equity shareholders? The latter just irritates your stockholders. The former gives bond holders the power to put you out of business. A stock offering is certainly the lesser of the two evils. Certainly, such actions have raised the bond prices for these companies.

Don't be fooled. There's a cycle to balance sheet leverage. The de-leveraging trend is just temporary. It may well last a few years. However, as soon as the economy turns around and these same companies can once again issue debt without paying an arm and a leg, they will. Then they'll be back up to pre-crisis leverage ratios. This is how balance sheet repair turns into balance sheet despair.

It's not enough for bondholders to recognize problems in the executive suite. A look at the bigger picture can identify systemic issues with an entire industry. Chapter 7, Bond Rating Agencies, is a part of that bigger picture. It shows how the rating agencies served as enablers for bond issuers that never should have carried the golden ratings they did. Equally as important, it shows how to spot such systemic problems before you own them.

The Bond Rating Agencies

Their names were positively legendary: Moody's Investor Services, Standard & Poor's, and Fitch Ratings. Their reputations for detailed, thorough analysis and independent opinion were equaled only by the Final Four public accounting firms. Most business contracts involving securities referenced a minimum rating that came from at least two of these firms. State and federal government relied on their ratings. Municipalities courted their favor when issuing bonds since even a single down-tick in their rating could cost millions in added interest expense. Their revenues soared into the billions.

Yet they played a vital role in almost bringing down the U.S.' entire economic system. They rated over a trillion dollars of bonds and other securities it turned out didn't deserve those high ratings. Investors relied on those ratings and lost more than just their shirts. They lost their retirement money, their nest eggs, and many elderly people lost their financial independence.

Once Highly Regarded

These are big companies. Moody's, the only one of the three that stands alone as a publicly traded company, has averaged pretax profit margins of 52 percent over the past five years. Last year Moody's reported revenue of $1.73 billion. Even during the economic collapse of 2008 Moody's earned an operating margin of 42 percent and threw 25 percent to the bottom line. Both Standard & Poor's and Fitch are said to enjoy similar profit margins.

Limited competition leads to very high fees. S&P, Moody's, and Fitch control 98 percent of the market for debt ratings in the United States, according to the SEC. These three rating companies were supposed to provide independent judgment on the safety of bond instruments issued by corporations, states, and a variety of municipalities. A single letter downgrade or even a plus or minus sign after one of their ratings was worth big money, depending on the bond issue size.

How could this have happened? Three reasons: The rating agencies were too big; there was no competition for the business; and there was too much reliance on their product by people who should have known better. Today, most bondholders wish they had never heard of Moody's, Standard & Poor's, or Fitch. Their ratings—at least of the bond insurance companies—are today largely ignored in favor of the issuer's underlying financial statements.

Flawed from the Start

Even a noncompetitive industry like bond rating is driven by money. All three rating agencies received money from those companies and municipalities they rated. It's an inherent conflict of interest. To outsiders it appeared that if raters wanted to keep the issuer as an ongoing client, it gave the issuer the rating it needed to float the bond. This created a flawed rating system from the very beginning.

Of course, the agencies tried to mitigate such charges. No single client accounted for a material amount of their total revenue. The analytical division had a built-in Chinese wall separating them from the sales division. But what about their relationships with major referral sources? Say a single investment bank was responsible for referring a rating agency 25 percent of its annual total revenues. How could investors know where those clients came from? Were the ratings on issuers coming from such a huge source of business any more favorable than the others? There is simply no way to tell. Because there's no way to tell, the ratings are clouded.

Edmund Vogelius, a Moody's vice president, wrote an article back in 1957 where he clearly stated the problem of independence:

> We obviously cannot ask payment for rating a bond. To do so would attach a price to the process, and we could not escape the charge, which would undoubtedly come, that our ratings are for sale.

This is not new. The financial industry is replete with such conflicts. CPA firms receive fees from those very companies they audit. Securities analysts publish their findings on the same companies and municipalities that their employers—the broker/dealers and investment bankers—are pedaling to their clients. Insurance companies do the underwriting on customers who buy their insurance.

One solution for the rating industry is for the investors to pay for production of the ratings, not the issuers. This guarantees thorough, thoughtful, and independent assessment. Will it happen? Probably not.

So What Happened?

The bond rating agencies were a victim of their own success. So much reliance was placed on their ratings by so many bond issuers and investors that soon their ratings could literally move entire markets. That was their downfall. Their executives became afraid to make the tough decisions early for fear it would anger their clients. Instead, they waited much too long. When they finally did issue overdue downgrades, they caused panic in the markets.

The rating agency's decline began when they rated the bond insurance companies—called the monoline insurers because they insured just one thing, municipal bonds. For years there was no problem. AMBAC, MBIA, Radian, FGIC, and the others insured billions in municipal debt. On those rare occasions when a municipal issuer defaulted, the insurance claims were small and manageable. The monoliners had plenty of cash reserves to honor their insurance claims. There was no question that they would maintain their AAA rating.

When a municipal bond issue came to market, the rating agencies rated the issuer. However, the bond issue was usually insured by MBIA, AMBAC, or the others. The rating agencies had already rated the insurance company. In the event of a default, investors would look to the insurance company to be made whole. So what real meaning did the underlying rating of the actual issuer have? Who cares if they can't pay the debt service? The insurance companies will pony up the cash if need be.

The rating agencies probably asked themselves, "Why spend all that time and money conducting analytical procedures and due diligence proceedings on some bond issuer that carries insurance from a top-rated company? Instead, let's ratchet down the scope of our work on the issuer and boost our profit margins."

Essentially, the rating agencies began relying on the underwriting work of the bond insurers to determine their issuer ratings. After all, if this issuer is good enough for AMBAC or MBIA, it's good enough for us.

Their death knell came when the rating agencies branched out into the new derivative markets of collateralized debt obligations and mortgage-backed securities. Beneath these lurked the quicksand of sub-prime loans. The rating agencies knew the risk of being wrong had increased. What they failed to grasp was by how much and what trouble the housing market was headed for. They probably told each other:

> There are a lot more players in the structured securities game. And it seems more complicated, though who could ever really understand these things anyway?

S&P, Moody's, and Fitch were able to charge on average three times more in fees for grading structured securities than they could for rating ordinary bonds.

> Still, they're insured by our old friends AMBAC, MBIA, Radian, and the rest of the gang. These guys all carry AAA ratings. We said so in our ratings, didn't we? So what's the risk?

The rating agencies applied the same limited scope of procedures to the structured securities so long as they were insured. They never imagined how overextended in potential claims their precious insurers were in case these structured securities took a dive.

The stress tests both the insurance companies and the rating agencies applied proved much too shallow. That is, the mathematical models they use to project required cash reserves needed to settle insurance claims in the event of a market downturn fell too far short of the Armageddon that was actually experienced. Who knew?

It was mid-2007 when investors learned the extent of the sub-prime problem. The collateralized mortgage and mortgage securities markets were jammed with this worthless debt. Both markets began to crumble. Financial firms around the world reported total write-offs approaching $1.3 trillion. Most of these were insured.

What were the monoliners to do? They didn't have that kind of cash in reserve to pay off such claims. The CEOs of both AMBAC and MBIA went to the news media claiming there was no problem with their cash reserves. Nothing could have been further from the truth. They began raising capital as if their lives depended on it. In fact, only meeting the rating agencies' AAA rating requirements depended on it.

What the public failed to grasp was that a downgrade of the insurance company ratings would immediately translate to an equivalent downgrade of the structured debt and the billions in unrated municipal bonds that were wrapped in insurance and for which the insurance companies were liable. It was a house of cards. When the rating downgrades finally began, the value of all the insured debt tanked. Investors would lose hundreds of billions, perhaps trillions.

What did the venerable ratings agencies do? They owed the investment public who relied on their opinion an answer. But they would be blamed for not seeing how overextended the monoliners were and failing to downgrade them sooner. What did they do? Nothing.

Meanwhile the stock price of the big insurers—AMBAC, MBIA, Radian, and FGIC—all dropped like a stone (see Figures 7.1 and 7.2).

Notice the rapid decline in the stock price of the two biggest bond insurers. To the most casual observer this would raise questions. But, still no downgrades from the rating agencies. It wasn't until the very end that the rating agencies finally began to downgrade their insurance company clients. Like the man in the picture, they tried in vain to keep their heads in the sand, hoping this all would just somehow go away.

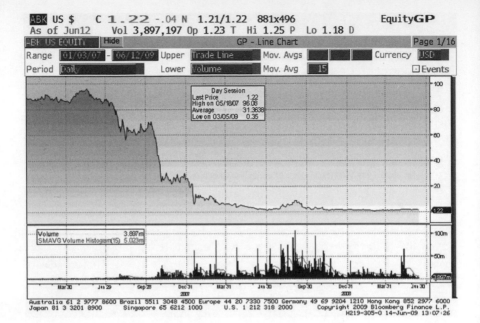

Figure 7.1 AMBAC Stock Chart

Source: Bloomberg Finance L.P. © 2009 Bloomberg Finance L.P. All rights reserved.
Used with permission.

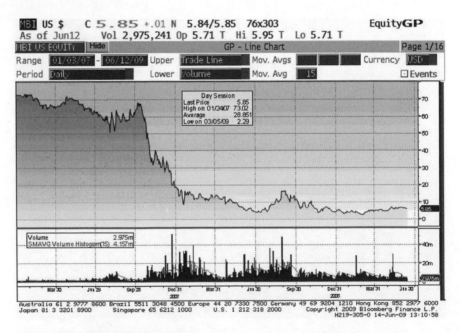

Figure 7.2 MBIA Stock Chart

Source: Bloomberg Finance L.P. © 2009 Bloomberg Finance L.P. All rights reserved.
Used with permission.

Windfall at Taxpayer's Expense

Certainly, the rating agencies had a great deal to do with the economic meltdown of 2008. Yet they are now poised to profit handsomely from the additional work sponsored by the Fed's financial rescue plan. Connecticut Attorney General Richard Blumenthal predicts the rating agencies could get as much as $400 million in fees coming from taxpayer money.

Meaning of Ratings

The Standard & Poor's AAA rating (or its equivalent Aaa from Moody's or AAA from Fitch) once meant the bond was safe from default. Not anymore. The credibility of the rating agencies has come under the microscope. Now, more than ever, investors must rely on their own analysis and judgment of the issuer's capacity to service the debt—the so-called underlying rating.

Still, an investment grade credit rating from the three large rating agencies provides some guidance that the municipality will likely repay its interest and principal as the bond indenture promises. Use it only as a guideline to corroborate other information pointing in the same direction. Table 7.1 shows what the ratings mean, from investment grade to junk.

The lower down the rating chain, the higher a bond's yield must be to attract investors and compensate them for the added risk.

 Action Step: Don't Trust the Ratings

Don't base your investment decisions solely on ratings. They may be wrong. They may be getting ready to issue a downgrade that is months late in coming. Such errors have cost investors tens of billions.

Importance of Ratings

Securities ratings figure in most buy/sell decisions in the bond market. Reference to ratings and restrictions on what can be bought guide money managers throughout the world's financial system. For example, the Federal Reserve's Term Asset-Backed Securities Loan Facility (TALF) will finance the purchase by taxpayers of as much

Table 7.1   Ratings from the Three Rating Agencies

	Moody's	S&P	Fitch
Prime, maximum safety	Aaa	AAA	AAA
High grade, high quality	Aa1	AA+	AA+
	Aa2	AA	AA
	Aa3	AA−	AA−
Upper medium grade	A1	A+	A+
	A2	A	A
	A3	A−	A−
Medium grade	Baa1	BBB+	BBB+
	Baa2	BBB	BBB
	Baa3	BBB−	BBB−
Speculative or junk grade	Ba	BB+	BB+
		BB	BB
		BB−	BB−
	B	B+	B+
		B	B
		B−	B−
	Caa	CCC+	CCC+

as $1 trillion of new securities backed by consumer loans or other asset-backed debt—*only on the condition they have triple-A ratings.* One trillion dollars. What if the ratings are wrong? What if just one of the rating agency's analytical models is wrong?

Way back in 1991 the SEC ruled that money market mutual fund managers must put 95 percent of their investments into highly rated commercial paper. The Fed has also been buying commercial paper directly from companies since October. Not just any commercial paper. Only that paper *carrying the equivalent of an A-1 rating,* the second highest for short-term credit. Keep in mind, the rating for this huge investment of taxpayer money came from the very same three rating companies that gave Lehman Brothers debt a rating of A-1 on the day it filed for bankruptcy.

Reference to debt grades are baked into hundreds of rules, laws, and private contracts that affect banking, insurance, mutual funds, and pension funds. U.S. Securities and Exchange Commission guidelines require money market fund managers to rely on ratings in deciding what to buy with $3.9 trillion of investors' money.

State insurance regulators depend on credit grades to monitor the safety of $450 billion of bonds held by U.S. insurance companies. Even the economic stimulus plans crafted by Federal Reserve Chairman Bernanke and Treasury Secretary Geithner count on rating firms to determine on what securities the money will be spent.

It wasn't until September 2008 before Moody's and S&P downgraded insurance giant AIG to A2 and A–. These were still the sixth and seventh highest investment grade ratings. AIG had insured an enormous amount of collateralized debt obligations and was knee-deep in credit default swaps. The downgrade was AIG's death knell. Their insurance contracts had a ratings floor. Any rating at or below A2 or A– triggered insurance payouts. When AIG couldn't come up with the cash, the U.S. government had to front AIG $85 billion to stave off mass fiscal panic. The government has since more than doubled AIG's rescue funds.

Not All Smooth Sailing

Congress has held hearings on credit raters. The first came after the Enron debacle. They've been held every year through 2008. Congress even passed the Credit Rating Agency Reform Act in 2006 giving the SEC limited authority to regulate raters' business practices. Then in December 2008 the SEC adopted rules that banned rating firms from grading debt structures they designed themselves.

By then the horse was out of the barn. The rating agencies helped design and then rated the two biggest toxic contributors to the U.S.' economic collapse: Collateralized debt obligations and mortgages.

It is now obvious that the analytical methods and mathematical models used by the rating agencies left much to be desired. However, the 2008 law expressly forbids the SEC from ordering the rating firms to change their analytical methods. The SEC was late to the party. When they finally did arrive, their rules were without the necessary teeth to do any good. Go figure.

The Perfect Storm of Financial Crisis

The rating agencies contributed mightily to the U.S.' financial crisis, but they didn't cause it. The problems were a combination of circumstances. Had each occurred separately at different times, our nation would have weathered the storm. They didn't. Instead, they piled on, one atop the other to create a perfect economic storm. Here's what happened:

1. The banks begin selling home mortgages to people who could not otherwise qualify. The banks were not at risk since they sold these mortgages to Freddie Mac, Fannie Mae, various hedge funds, and institutional investors. The banks got to keep the origination and servicing fees but without the risk of holding the debt and hoping the debtors would pay off.

2. The home mortgages were bundled into pools (securitized) and sold as publicly traded securities called collateralized mortgage obligations (CMOs). CMOs and some collateralized debt obligations (CDOs) were insured by the major monoline agencies. The rating agencies bestowed the same rating they gave to the insurance companies on the CMOs and CDOs—usually the top investment grade. The banks decide to keep many of the securities, leverage them to the hilt and earn the interest carry.

3. The economy turned downward and jobs were lost.

4. The toxic sub-prime mortgages the banks sold (see #1) began defaulting in vast numbers.

5. Home foreclosures flooded the market, creating an enormous glut of unsold property.

6. The banks stopped lending for fear of further weakening their capital positions.

7. This oversupply with almost zero demand caused the floor to fall out from under housing prices.

8. The massive mortgage default caused the underlying mortgage securities pools to default. The insurance companies that guaranteed these securities did not have sufficient reserves to honor the claims presented.

9. The banks had no choice but to write down hundreds of billions of dollars in these securities and feverishly try to plug the holes.

10. The write-downs compromised the bank's capital structure, which placed them on the edge of failing.

11. This caused a consolidation in the banking industry with the stronger banks buying the weaker ones.

12. Fannie Mae and Freddie Mac, owners and issuers of these now deeply discounted securities, sustained huge losses. So huge that they compromised their core capital.
13. The U.S. government placed Freddie and Fannie into a conservatorship. They were too big and too important to the banking system to fail. Without them the banks would never lend on a new mortgage that they couldn't sell to Freddie or Fannie.
14. The U.S. government stepped in, demanding banks take their TARP funds. This was the de facto nationalization of the U.S. banking system the pundits were complaining about.

What Now?

The rating agencies have so tarnished their reputations and credibility that the financial community no longer respects them. Like a suspect interrogated under duress, the rating agencies have said anything to restore investor confidence in their product. After all, they can always recant later. Their mission—and that of their CEOs—is to get the financial markets back on the old program of paying for their ratings.

Surprisingly, it's not such a hard sell. Ratings are so entrenched and pervasive in the financial industry that even now most investors use them. Ratings are like a drug. The financial industry is addicted to them to one degree or another.

To their credit, the rating agencies have made some significant changes to salvage their reputations and their businesses. The structured finance departments that were asleep at the switch are now disbanded. The corporate and municipal bond analysis departments are still in place and somewhat credible. It will take time for the market to forget the rating agencies' past transgressions and grant its former confidence in their opinions. The agencies' downgrades now come faster and are more punitive than ever before in history. In this case, the threat of government intervention has done its job. Additionally, this experience has strengthened the rating agency's monitoring and alarm systems for fiscal problems in corporate and municipal bonds.

There has been a change in culture at Moody's, Standard & Poor's, and Fitch. The rotten wood has been replaced with more competent analysts and managers. But can you trust their ratings?

Not like before. Many bond investors once started and ended their analysis using just the rating. Only those with their heads still in the sand would do that again.

Use the ratings only as a guide. Instead, rely on your personal analysis (see Chapter 11, Bond Analysis, to see how it's done). Study the bond and make your own judgment rather than trusting anyone else with your money. The cyclicality of bull market greed comes and goes many times throughout an investor's career. The 2008 meltdown was just one very deep trough in the cycle. Study and learn the lessons that overreliance on bond ratings teach. Don't make the same mistake again and you'll be fine.

Coming up in Chapter 8, How to Buy and Sell Bonds, you get to apply these lessons. You'll learn how the bond market has adopted a new set of rules. They're not written anywhere in the government regulations. Nevertheless, savvy investors know how to use the new system to their own advantage.

How to Buy and Sell Bonds

WITHOUT BEING TAKEN TO THE CLEANERS

Buying bonds can be intimidating. Especially if your broker is busy and doesn't have the time to hold your hand. Just remember, you are the customer. Your bond broker works for you. If he doesn't, then he shouldn't be your broker for long. The problem comes when individual investors allow the broker to take over the transaction. As the customer, your mission is to get exactly which bond you want at or near the price you specified. That's how individual investors make money in Bondland. Otherwise, why come to the dance in the first place? Your broker's priority is different. He is there to put as much of your cash into his pocket in as little time as possible. See the difference in priorities?

Chapter 8 shows you how to take command of your bond transactions. There are just a few easy steps to follow that will:

- Help you determine exactly which type of bond you need in your portfolio.
- Enable you to stick to a written investment discipline that is uniquely yours.
- Avoid buying bonds whose risk exceeds what you're comfortable with and can afford.
- Tell your broker what's on your shopping list rather than taking what he has to offer.
- Establish your price range for a bond and get it at a price within that range.

- Show you how to negotiate bond transactions on an equal footing with your broker.

This is truly the art of bond investing. We professional money managers use each of these techniques every business day. You should too. When done the right way, not only is bond investing profitable, it's fun too. You are in command and have seized control over the transaction. What's not fun about that? On the other hand, ignoring these steps can be extraordinarily costly. Let's get started.

Be a Bond Collector

Some people collect stamps, some collect watches. Individual bond investors collect bonds. Just as a stamp collector targets specific issues, countries, and eras, bond collectors also have specific holes to fill in their collections. That's why bond investors buy and sell their bonds. They may need a particular maturity to fill a hole in their maturity ladder. They may need a municipal bond issued by their state of residence to generate tax-exempt income. They may need to sell a bond that looks like its issuer is about to be downgraded to a level that no longer fits their risk profile. All are valid reasons to execute a bond trade.

Figuring out what you need (and no longer need) in your bond collection is half the battle. Remember *El Greedo* from Chapter 5? It cost *El* $1 million to learn how to buy and sell bonds. In the end he finally got it. A costly education to be sure. However, without learning the collector's discipline, *El* would have likely lost more.

Action Step: Bond Selection

No self-respecting stamp collector would ever leave selection of his next purchase up to a stamp salesman. Same thing with bonds. Never leave selection of the type of bond to the broker. He likely doesn't know what's already in your bond portfolio. Further, he couldn't care less if you achieve your fixed income investment goals. Selling a bond to a customer means the broker won't see that money again for years, whereas with equities he can rotate customers in and out of stocks all year long and generate a continuing stream of commissions.

Allowing the broker to sell you a bond puts you in a passive role. We professionals never take a passive role when trading bonds. Neither should you. Acting as the participating, engaged buyer makes all the difference. As the bond investor, you want to be an integral part of *your* transaction. Be a proactive buyer.

Select specific bonds to do a particular job in your portfolio. For some it may be a steady, stable income stream. For others it is safety of principal. Other bonds in your portfolio offer some upside potential in the event interest rates fall.

When *El Greedo* rebalanced his portfolio, he knew just where he wanted to allocate his bond investments. A certain percentage was going to the energy sector, the food sector, the retail sector, and so on. Within those sectors he chose specific companies that met his criteria. Within those companies he went on to select particular maturities to guarantee him the income stream he needed. He knew exactly what bonds he needed to fill in his collection. When *El* picked up the phone to call his broker, the conversation was pretty one sided:

El: "I need 50 Conagra Notes 5.875% due April 15, 2014. CUSIP number is 205887BE1. Here's my bid."

Broker: "Good morning to you too, Mr. Greedo. Yes sir, Mr. Greedo, I'll see what I can do."

This is the difference between a savvy investor who is buying what he needs versus someone who is shopping and willing to be sold whatever the broker has on the shelf at the time. Now, *El* already knew the price at which his bonds were trading from looking at the TRACE system. That's how he knew where to bid. We'll show you the mechanics of TRACE later in this chapter. Additionally, he will have the same conversation with at least one other broker. Further, *El* has already decided to walk if the market runs away from his bid (rises too far above the bid).

The value your broker adds to the deal and the reason why he earns his commissions with a savvy investor—opposed to taking his commission from a less astute investor—is in working the transaction. He may be unable to find the Conagra bonds at the price *El* specified. He will likely recommend another bond in the same sector with relatively the same yield and maturity date that he can get. His worth as a broker lies in his ability to hit your bid with a fair price and do it quickly.

You know your bond collection and requirements better than your broker. Therefore, you should be the one telling the broker what you will buy.

Stick to Your Investment Discipline

Successful bond investors have a disciplined approach to managing their portfolio. This is not usually a person's play money that's on the line. Further, that money and the importance of what it is used for leaves little margin for error. That's why the first step in buying and selling bonds is to establish the investment discipline that works for you and stick to it.

Investment Discipline Defined

El Greedo once was an undisciplined investor. He bought bonds for their yield alone as long as they were in the one sector he thought he understood—financials. That's not how a disciplined bond investor rolls.

Think of your bond investment discipline as a code of conduct. You don't deviate from it without a very good reason. When you do, you will always return to the discipline.

Here are the criteria to use when selecting the bonds for inclusion in your portfolio.

Sector   Identify the industries and businesses with which you want to populate your bond portfolio. There will be some sectors you think are stable and will continue to be so. There are others that you see as containing upside potential as the economy crawls out of its recession. Sectors to avoid will be those you think are poised for a correction.

Keep in mind you're not necessarily always looking for capital appreciation. Instead you want an issuer that will continue to pay bond interest and principal and perhaps at least maintain the bond's value.

Bond Issuers   The issuers are the particular companies and municipalities within a sector. Part of an investment discipline related to issuers often has to do with minimum underlying ratings, minimum debt coverage, and cash flow.

Maturity   Staggering maturities is important. It calibrates your duration and interest rate risk. Also, knowing when to sell is the most difficult decision for every investor. By staggering maturities in a laddered portfolio you won't have to decide when to sell a given bond. The bonds mature and roll off every few years automatically. Further, should there be a significant upward move in interest rates, driving down bond values, you know you won't have to take the pain forever. Your laddered maturities roll off in an orderly manner.

Rolling down the yield curve is a term that pertains to maturity. Say you buy an eight-year bond. But after two years, interest rates rise. Where does that leave you? The eight-year bond has now become a six year bond. As you get closer to maturity, your bond value will move less in response to a change in interest rates. Therefore, the shorter the bond maturity, the less volatile the bond value.

Yield   Yield is a function of the coupon rate and the bond's price. As the bond price climbs, yield falls. Choose bonds whose price gets you the most yield for the risk and maturity you're willing to take. Decide if buying a premium or discount bond fits your yield needs.

Safety from Default   Many bond investors consider safety from default as part of their overall investment discipline. Perhaps not for the entire portfolio, but for at least a portion. For corporates, this is pretty much limited to the financial stability of the issuing company. We've all witnessed the horror of companies believed to be among the strongest come tumbling down. However, certain municipal bonds do afford complete safety from default. This is not bond insurance. Rather they are types of bonds such as:

- **PSF:** Texas' Permanent School Fund Guarantee program allows its school districts to issue bonds. If a district cannot pay bond interest and principal, the Texas PSF Commissioner transfers sufficient funds to meet the obligation.
- **Intercept bonds:** Twenty states provide financial support for school bond issuers. The actual program names vary but the guarantee is unwavering. If a local government cannot make a coupon or principle payment on its school bonds, the bond bank legally intercepts any funds held by the state treasurer that are payable to the bond issuer and pays them directly to the bond holders.
- **Double-barreled:** These are general obligation bonds of the issuer that are also secured by a particular revenue source outside the general fund. Should the first revenue source dry

up, then the general obligation general fund kicks in to pay interest and principal.

- **General obligation bonds:** Issued by states or municipalities with taxing authority, GO bondholders have first payment priority for use of state funds. There are exceptions. For example, California GOs sit behind school bonds in payment priority order.

- **Prerefunded bonds and bonds escrowed to maturity:** Prerefunded bonds (preres in Bondspeak) are simply bonds that the state or municipal issuer retired from its balance sheet and moved to an escrow account. They issue new bonds whose proceeds are used to retire the old bonds at the next call date or on maturity. The proceeds sit in an escrow account where the money is safely invested until the call date or maturity. Repayment is guaranteed by this escrow account.

Structure   Bond structure relates to the bond's principal and interest payments—how and when your money is repaid. For example, in a *step-up bond* the coupon steps up—rises—after so many years. Alternatively, it can also fall should the bond's rating be downgraded. This is a way of helping the issuer early in the bond's life while compensating the buyers later for the risk they took and forbearance they exercised. We don't recommend step-up bonds and will explain why later.

Structured bonds are something different. They link the bond's interest rate to an index using a derivative. For example, a credit-linked note is a bond with an embedded credit derivative.

Inflation-adjusted bonds link the interest rate (or the principal for TIPS) to the consumer price index. This gives investors concerned about inflation some relief in the event their worry becomes reality.

Call Features   Many bonds limit the issuer's interest rate risk with the ability to call back the bond according to a pre-established feature. Select the bond with the call features you need such as non-callable, callable once, callable in five years and then every year thereafter, or some other combination. Some bonds have a premium payment payable to the bondholder should the bond be called before maturity. This *call protection* acts as partial compensation for foregone interest revenue should the bond be called.

Yield to Worst Call   Many corporate, government agency, and municipal bonds are callable. It is important to calculate the worst yield you will potentially earn. Here's an example of Valero Energy Corp. 7.50% due June 15, 2015, CUSIP 74047PAH7, callable. It was purchased on October 1, 2008 at 98. The Yield to Maturity is 7.89%. But wait. What is the Yield to Worst Call? This is the minimum you will get. Here's the call schedule:

- June 15, 2015 @ 101.25 gives a YTW of 9.48%
- June 15, 2011 @ 100 give a YTW of 8.33%

So the Yield to Worst Call is actually the Yield to Maturity, 7.89%—the lowest yield of the three.

Deviations from Investment Discipline

Successful bond investors know when and how to deviate from their investment discipline. They have good reasons. They always return to their discipline when the temporary fling is over. Usually, the deviation occurs for a one-time opportunity.

For example, let's say your bond discipline allocates just 2 percent of the portfolio to financial issuers. Further, because of their problems during the 2008 credit meltdown you decide that the financial issuer rating should not be below Aaa2 by Moody's.

Then you hear about Jefferies Group, stock ticker JEF. Jefferies is a full-service broker/dealer that does investment banking. It doesn't package, inventory, or sell CDOs. Nor does it traffic in credit default swaps. You notice that most analysts dislike Jefferies' stock. You read their reports saying, "the fixed income trading business lacks visibility. Investment banking is depressed. Competition is difficult."

But now, being a savvy bond investor, you tell yourself, "All that bad news certainly must already be baked into their bond price." Next, you look up Jefferies bond trading history on TRACE. You see numerous small trades: 25's, 50s, and 120s, whereas, the large blocks of 500 thousand, a million, or more are nowhere to be found. You conclude that the institutional bond boys have overlooked Jefferies.

Someone has missed the boat. Jefferies isn't huge. But it has a niche and has outlasted the big names like Citi, JP Morgan, and Bank of America. These giants tried to become all things to all investors. They only succeeded in blowing so many holes in their balance sheets it made Swiss cheese look solid. All the investigations of these big banks by the enforcement authorities probably tainted the sector.

You decide to deviate from your investment discipline and nibble on a $25,000 schnitzel of the Jefferies Group Senior Unsecured 5.50% due March 15, 2016 (CUSIP 472319AB8). These bonds carry a Moody's rating of Baa2, which is below your minimum rating of Aaa2. Further, you are now overweight in your allocation to the financial sector. Still, the issue size is $350 million so there should be sufficient liquidity to get out if you need to. You bid 86 for the bonds, which gives you a yield to maturity of a whopping 8.25 percent.

This deviation from your investment discipline is a risk. Making a habit of such departures would probably not be a good thing. Still, you did your homework. You applied logic to a fluid situation and made a well-calculated decision. Now you go back to employing your investment discipline until the next departure.

Establish Your Risk Profile *(and Stick to It)*

With bonds, you're actually buying a stream of cash flows. You are betting the issuer can maintain that stream of cash flows over the entire maturity period of the bond. This can be 5, 10, 20 years, or longer. For corporate bonds you buy the company and its management. For municipal bonds you buy the category (GO, Revenue), their reserves, and, if they ever had to dip into them, their track record and the state they're in for income tax purposes.

Bond risk has many components. The fact is, most everything associated with a bond affects risk. The bond investor's job is to put all these variables into a funnel and distill the results into an assessment of the risk that the bonds will continue to pay interest and principal on maturity.

Determiners of Risk

Here's a partial list of the components bond professionals look at when assessing a bond's risk to determine if it fits into a portfolio:

1. **Transparency:** Does the municipality voluntarily file its financial statements for you to study? If not, then you're totally blind as to the issuer's financial stability.
2. **Rating:** Many prudent corporate bond investors have a minimum rating of BBB as a component of their investment

discipline. This sometimes requires investors to sell bonds that are downgraded to less than BBB to maintain their investment discipline.

3. **Underlying rating:** This is the municipal bond rating without any insurance, purely the issuer's rating

4. **Payment guarantee:** This isn't insurance. Rather, it is the payment structure of the bond such as prerefunded, escrowed to maturity, double- barreled, or a GARVEE bond.

    We haven't talked about GARVEE bonds yet. GARVEEs are Grant Anticipation Revenue Vehicles, defined as financing instruments that allow states to fund their transportation projects based on anticipated payment of future highway funds. The interest and principal money source for GARVEE bonds comes from the Federal Highway Trust Fund that receives money from gas tax revenues then transfers it to the individual states. GARVEEs are considered relatively safe.

5. **Economy:** The overall economy is a factor, as is the geographic economy for municipal bonds.

6. **Creditworthiness:** Issuers should be able to borrow funds for operations.

7. **Size of the issue:** Issue size equates to liquidity—your ability to buy and sell the bond at your price when you need to. Without sufficient liquidity in a bond, your risk of holding it rises.

8. **Collateral:** Bonds are a debt. If it isn't repaid, the bondholders can force the issuer into bankruptcy. If there is good and sufficient collateral, the bondholders will be made whole. If not, or if the once good collateral suddenly becomes impaired, then the risk of holding the bonds just rose.

9. **Management:** Look for a stable management in lower risk bonds. If the management team appears unstable or if it has a lot of new, untested members, then your risk has increased.

Any one of these risk items can throw a bond outside of an investor's risk profile if it is significant enough.

Form a Shopping List

At this stage in your bond buying and selling, you've done your homework. The hard part is over. You've become a bond collector, knowing what each bond in your portfolio must do to reach your overall goal. You've come up with an investment discipline. You've defined all sorts of things about your bond portfolio. You know the sectors you'll invest in; what issuers make sense for you; the maturities you need to establish your duration and interest rate risk; the yields you need that give you sufficient income; what safety levels you're comfortable with; the structure of the bonds you need in your collection; the overall risk profile you want for your portfolio; you know when you're willing to deviate from this investment discipline.

Bond shopping is the fun part. Now you get to enter the marketplace and buy the bonds you need to fill the holes in your collection and sell those bonds that no longer fit.

 Action Step: Bond Description

Unless you're a bond professional, you probably won't know which bonds you need to buy according to their CUSIP number. That's okay. Instead, you can very precisely define the attributes of your target bond and give your minimum of two brokers the assignment of finding it. Give your brokers the industry sector, maturity needed to fill in your maturity ladder and fine tune your duration, the yield to maturity, coupon desired, and the amount of your investment. That should be enough to get them started in their search. The search is their job. Pit them against one another. It's competition, dear readers.

For example, when *El Greedo* finally bought the Best Buy Inc. Notes 6.75% Due July 15, 2013, shown on his rebalanced portfolio in Chapter 5, he didn't know that was the bond he wanted. Even so, he knew a lot about it from the solid homework he did on his collection. He was able to tell his brokers everything about his target bond that they needed to know to find it. Here's how that conversation went:

Broker: "Yes sir, Mr. Greedo. What can I get for you today?"
El: "Yeah. Got a $25,000 hole here I need to fill in my retail sector."
Broker: "Great. It just so happens I have—"
El: "No, you don't. Just listen. And take a note. Here's what I want you to get me. I need $25,000 of a niche retailer in the consumer electronics space. Make sure they have something special that separates them from the herd, will ya? I

need a company that's ready to grab market share to ensure their stability. I don't want a management that's new to the company or the industry. They should be bond friendly. No dumb-ass stock buy-back programs funded by debt. Understand? The rating—make it no less than BBB. I want a stable balance sheet. You know my minimum interest coverage ratio. I want a good-sized issue—no less than $250 million in case I need to dump it quick. Got all that?"

Broker: "Yes sir, Mr. Greedo. I sure do want to tell you about the healthcare bonds we have in inventory though."

El: "You got 'em in inventory means you need to dump 'em. Not interested in the healthcare sector. Call me when you come up with something in my consumer electronics retailer." Click.

Admittedly *El* is a crusty character. What can we say? The auto parts business is a tough industry. *El* ran with the big dogs. Still, there was no question in that conversation as to who was in control. *El* is the customer, and he knows what he needs in his bond portfolio.

His broker came up with the Best Buy idea. It fit all of *El's* demands. Best Buy is one of the leading big box consumer electronics retailers. Its acquisition of the firm that became their Geek Squad provides a unique and profitable twist to the businesses. It makes the complicated electronics that the stores sell less intimidating for the customers. Best Buy is grabbing market share especially from the Circuit City (now bankrupt) customers. They have a solid, stable management team. The balance sheet and their interest coverage meet *El's* requirements.

The rating is BBB– though. This is a slight deviation from *El's* minimum BBB. Because Best Buy met all his other requirements, *El* decided to make a slight deviation from his investment discipline. Especially since he discovered there's a chance that Best Buy's rating could be upgraded shortly. Last, the issue size of the bonds *El* is looking at was $500 million—double his minimum size.

The second broker wasn't listening to *El* and lamely came up with Nordstrom 6.75% due June 1, 2014. Although Nordstrom has a good balance sheet, it is in apparel, not electronics. It has a stable management but it has already elbowed its competitors out of business. Who is left to grab market share from? Nobody.

The bond issue is $400 million. But *El's* other requirements weren't satisfied by broker #2. The broker ignored *El's* detailed road map. Broker #2 doesn't get the order. If this happens too often, *El* will replace him.

That's how you create a bond shopping list and broker competition to fill your orders. It is very specific in its requirements. It gives the brokers a detailed road map of what exactly you want. They're willing to do the research because they know that you will buy the bonds that meet your requirements. It is time well spent for them.

How to Set Your Price

Finding the market price of most corporate and municipal bonds isn't difficult. Just access the Trade Reporting and Compliance Engine (TRACE). TRACE was developed by and uses trade data supplied by the Financial Industry Regulatory Authority (FINRA). You can access TRACE from the comfort of you own computer. It is free. Just go to the web site, www.investingingbonds.com. Click on the top menu option for bond markets and prices. Find the bond category you're interested in and type in the descriptive data or CUSIP number of your bond if you know it. TRACE will provide the recent prices at which your bond has traded.

Ignoring the critical price information found in TRACE would be like driving blindfolded in the fog. If you don't use TRACE, then you should not be trading the secondary market. Instead, buy a bond fund. All institutional traders use TRACE: bond funds, institutions trading desks, insurance companies. So why not you? Did we mention that it's free?

Armed with the most recent price information, set a range of prices at which you are willing to buy or sell your bond. These will provide you the yield that you are looking for. Then call up your brokers—at least two of them—and set your bid or offer. Don't make it a secret that you use TRACE and know the market for your bond. This saves a lot of time for you both since the brokers are less likely to test you with a price that is off the market.

The broker will give you a price within your range. You'll accept it. The broker will confirm by saying, "You're done at." The transaction is completed at your price. What could be easier than that?

Paying Up

Sometimes investors pay a higher price than the prevailing market for a similar bond. It is called paying up for a bond. This means that you accept less yield and pay a higher price than has been printed on TRACE. Why would you do that? For a corporate bond, you may really want to own that particular company. Your bond collection may need its diversification and its industry. For example, Wal-Mart has a lower yield and higher price than Target. If you want the best of breed, you'll buy Wal-Mart, even though it's priced higher than Target.

Paying up for municipal bonds may get you additional safety features. The safer the bond, the higher the price and lower the yield. For example, prerefunded bonds, bonds that are escrowed to maturity, double-barreled bonds, and GARVEE bonds that we introduced earlier are all safer than comparable bonds without their guarantees. Yes, they are more expensive and their yields aren't quite as juicy as their counterparts. But they do have the safety thing going for them. If your bond collection needs a certain percentage that is absolutely safe, then you are willing to sacrifice some yield for that comfort.

Working Three Different Markets

Many bond investors consider only the secondary market when they think of buying and selling bonds. Certainly, that's a primary market. We'll discuss that. But first, there's the new issue market to consider.

New Issues

When a new municipal bond is floated by an issuer, it first comes on the new issue market. Individual investors can buy new issues through their brokerage firm as long as they have access to the new issue. This means they're either a member of the underwriting group or the selling group. Most large brokerage firms have access to the new issue market. It's important that at least one of your brokers have new issue access. Only in the new issue market are bond prices not negotiated. The price stated is the price as a new issue.

When newly issued municipal bonds first come to market, some may have a retail order period. This is a period of a day or two where only retail orders from individual investors are taken. The retail order period applies only to municipal bonds. New issue corporate bonds do not have retail order periods. For municipal bonds, during the retail order period you won't have to compete with the big institutions to get the bonds you want. Once the retail order period expires, then the new issue market opens up to everyone, individuals and institutions alike.

To get in on the new issue retail order period just call your broker and ask what municipal bonds are available in the category you need from the new issue market. Ask to get into the retail order period. The broker will tell you what he can get and the price. You say *done*.

Secondary Market

When buying on the secondary market, you are buying from someone who already owns the bond and wishes to sell. Alternatively, if you're selling the bond, your broker needs to find a buyer willing to take it off your hands. It may be another retail customer, an institution, or his own inventory. Here are your steps to buy a bond on the secondary market:

1. Select the category and specifications of the bond your collection needs. Be as specific as possible and always include the CUSIP number if you have it.
2. Check prices on TRACE and arrive at a range of prices you are willing to bid for the bond. Your broker probably won't be able hit your target price exactly. But he should be able to get pretty close.
3. Call the broker and tell him what you want to buy and the price you want. The broker may say that he can't get the bonds, but he has something similar. Or he may say that he has the bonds but the price is higher than your bid.

    Listen to what your broker says, and then make your decision. Or go to your other broker. If the alternate bond is acceptable from a price and yield, rating, sector, and all the other attributes you're looking for, you may *lift the offering* (bond-speak for buy it). If the broker has priced the bond too high, you can pass. This is why you always have at least two brokers working your order. Each has different sources. Where one may fail to get a particular bond at your price, the other may succeed.

    The broker may also say he can get in touch with the bonds. This means he'll have his trading desk go find the bonds. The broker buys from someone else, marks them up, then sells them to you. Watch the price carefully in this case. There are often a lot fingers in this pie:

- First, there's the mark-up between the trading desk at your brokerage firm and the broker who has the bonds.
- Next there's a mark-up from your brokerage firm's trading desk to your broker.
- Finally, there's the mark-up from your broker to you.
- You can see these fingerprints reflected in off-the-market prices reported on TRACE.

All these mark-ups raise the price to you unless you negotiate. Don't be afraid to bid back on the price your broker says. Just because he says a price doesn't mean it's cast in stone. Try bidding back and see what he says. This process takes more time since the broker may have to run your counter bid back through the loop to see if all parties are willing to take less of a mark-up. In the end the deal either gets done at a price that you agree to or you walk.

Buying Bonds Online

The online market is no different mechanically from the secondary market described above. You can do limit orders specifying the maximum you'll pay—your bid. However, these bids won't usually get hit because all the mark-ups they carry take their price off market. Generally, the online market has a price for retail investors that is pretty firm. You take it or leave it.

Buying bonds online from a discount broker? There's no discount for bonds. *Nada, niet, nein, yox* (from the Azerbaijan bond exchange—kidding).

Buying bonds online is a win/win situation for the online platforms. The platform (Fidelity, Schwab, TD Ameritrade are just three) don't necessarily own the bonds. They offer someone else's bonds. They will always carry a mark-up. Remember that every mark-up takes a bite out of your yield.

Now that you know how to buy and sell bonds, let's use this knowledge to build a safe bond portfolio in Chapter 9.

CHAPTER 9

Managing Your Bond Portfolio

Moody's analyzed over 777,000 of the municipal bond ratings it conducted on 28,000 entities between 1970 and 2000. They found just 18 bond defaults. Ten of these were from hospitals. Then the credit crisis of 2008 hit. We didn't hear any credible default statistics before going to press. However, our guess is that there were significantly more than 18 bond defaults since 2008.

In the aftermath of the 2008 credit crisis it was impossible even for us bond market professionals to determine what was protected. Oh sure, Treasury bonds were the safe haven. But they returned nothing. Confidence was shaken because no other securities could be counted as safe. Not government agencies; not mortgage-backed securities; not corporate bonds. FDIC reserves were depleting fast due to bank closings. This eliminated the safety of bank bonds since banks couldn't issue bonds without the FDIC guarantee during the credit crisis. Fannie Mae and Freddie Mac preferred stock—once considered so safe that regional banks bought them to count toward their Tier 1 capital requirements—ceased paying the preferred dividend on command from the U.S. government. Their value almost went to zero.

The new world order in the bond market requires investors to manage their portfolios in a much different way than ever before. This section shows you what you need to know and what changes you need to make in order to manage a safe bond portfolio.

Maintain Flexibility

Simply stated: Don't be pig-headed. When you make an error in a bond admit it, bail out and move on. You'll find the pain of the loss diminishes over time. Remember the auto parts mogul, *El Greedo*? He once was pig-headed. The cure cost him a lot of money. But take the cure he did. Now his rebalanced portfolio is diversified and once again shows signs of life. *El* learned how to be flexible in the new bond market's rules of engagement. He changed from being a one-trick pony to managing a flexible, diversified portfolio.

Don't Flog a Loser

Say you bought non-rated municipal bonds wrapped with insurance and thought they were safe. Now you see the insurance company is teetering on the brink of insolvency. The bond no longer fits your risk criteria. Get out, if you can. Hoping you'll come out unscathed is for dreamers. Maybe you will; maybe you won't. Where once we might have been willing to take the chance, the new rules of engagement don't allow us to flog a loser.

Then there are the non-rated municipal bonds—such as special tax bonds and tax allocation bonds—issued by Stone & Youngberg and other small firms. These were insured by carriers that no longer have the resources to pay in the event of default. Investors were sold these bonds based only on their higher than normal yield. Remember our rule: There's a rate for every risk. Had investors proactively bought them for a specific strategic fit in their portfolio, they would have been in much better shape. Again, the remedy is to get out. Actually, the real solution is to never have gotten into them in the first place. Of course, no one knew it at the time.

Just look at Figure 9.1. It shows the states having insured bonds outstanding and what companies insured them. California leads the pack with $486.5 billion in municipal bonds outstanding. Of these, $250.95 billion are insured. But look what companies insured them. AMBAC isn't getting any business and is heading into the tank. National (formerly MBIA) has tons of litigation. FGIC is finished. FSA was purchased by Assured Guaranty, a solid insurer, so those bonds may be okay. Radian is finished. If you own any of the states bonds that are insured by these companies, better take a close look.

State	Outstanding[1]	Insured	AMBAC	NATL	FGIC	FSA	RADIAN	Other
CALIFORNIA	486.50	250.95	48.01	101.92	38.89	53.49	1.37	7.27
NEW YORK	321.36	117.34	21.22	44.20	18.41	27.51	0.87	5.13
TEXAS	279.97	93.19	19.53	33.39	12.69	21.57	2.57	3.45
FLORIDA	167.81	97.23	20.96	39.88	14.64	18.11	0.62	3.02
ILLINOIS	140.55	90.04	14.96	35.52	16.05	19.96	0.53	3.03
PENNSYLVANIA	135.55	72.64	12.95	20.03	11.00	23.78	1.29	3.59
NEW JERSEY	113.17	69.98	13.04	27.23	8.60	18.70	0.33	2.09
MASSACHUSETTS	92.58	39.69	9.23	13.60	4.26	10.68	0.38	1.55
OHIO	90.36	34.36	6.61	12.19	5.61	8.48	0.38	1.09
MICHIGAN	83.57	48.12	6.67	16.96	8.62	11.12	0.07	1.38
PUERTO RICO	79.87	25.67	5.88	9.17	4.58	4.74	0.00	1.30
GEORGIA	71.94	25.63	3.40	10.35	3.91	6.62	0.11	1.24
WASHINGTON	71.86	47.26	6.92	18.58	6.69	13.42	0.43	1.24
VIRGINIA	61.18	11.14	1.64	5.22	0.91	3.07	0.10	0.20
ARIZONA	57.41	25.03	4.50	10.03	5.43	4.42	0.07	0.57
COLORADO	56.83	30.63	1.30	12.53	3.16	7.63	0.91	1.01
N. CAROLINA	55.79	12.99	3.48	4.57	1.07	3.41	0.20	0.26
INDIANA	53.27	28.67	4.81	10.65	4.06	8.20	0.08	0.87
MINNESOTA	49.41	14.04	2.03	5.11	1.02	4.67	0.13	1.08
TENNESSEE	45.69	12.70	2.49	5.34	1.08	3.08	0.14	0.57

Amounts in $Billions

Australia 61 2 9777 8600 Brazil 5511 3048 4500 Europe 44 20 7330 7500 Germany 49 69 9304 1210 Hong Kong 852 2977 6000
Japan 81 3 3201 8900   Singapore 65 6212 1000   U.S. 1 212 318 2000   Copyright 2009 Bloomberg Finance L.P.
H219-305-0 28-Jun-09 12:55:09

Figure 9.1   MBT Insurers

Source: Bloomberg Finance L.P. © 2009 Bloomberg Finance L.P. All rights reserved. Used with permission.

Make a New Plan, Stan

Under the post-2008 credit crisis, investors can no longer just buy any corporate or municipal bonds and forget them. You need a well-defined plan for your overall bond portfolio. Make it the income-producing as well as the asset-protection engine of your investment strategy. We'll introduce the four most reliable bond investment strategies and how they work. Most successful investors use a combination of these four. If their holdings are large enough, many will segment their portfolio and apply one of the four to each segment. The point is to develop a plan you're happy with, implement it and give it a chance to do its job.

The four most reliable bond strategies are:

1. Passive investment that employs a buy and hold discipline.
2. Index matching, which is a modification of the passive discipline.

3. Immunization from outside influences with a targeted return.
4. Active strategy with the intent of maximizing the portfolio's total return.

Passive Bond Strategy—Not Like the Old Days

Don't think the passive strategy is one in which you can buy and forget. That's just its common moniker. This investment discipline seeks to build a safe portfolio that generates steady, reliable income. Using this strategy, we buy good quality corporates or municipal bonds without necessarily making any assumptions on the direction of interest rates or changes in the bonds' yields. We intend to hold them until maturity.

Consider the bonds you have in your passive discipline as the stable anchor for your portfolio during economic storms. Because we're holding them to maturity, we want investment grade corporates and very safe municipal bonds. The munis should be a combination of prerefunded, escrowed to maturity, PSF (public school fund), double-barreled, or GARVEE bonds. If you venture into other munis, make sure they are insured by no other carriers than Berkshire Hathaway Assurance or Assured Guaranty Ltd., which owns FSA. That way you don't have to worry about the interest and principal payments being made when they're due. We think these two insurance companies have the financial resources to make good on their promises.

Today's passive bond strategy is different from the passive strategy used before the 2008 credit crisis. That's because we now know the unthinkable can happen. What if U.S. Treasuries lose their AAA rating due to the horrific U.S. deficits? As master of your own portfolio, you will have to decide if AA U.S. Treasuries in an escrow account are a good enough credit quality for you.

What happens when Warren Buffett dies if his succession plan is as bad as Sandy Weill's (Citigroup), Jack Welch's (GE), or David Kamansky's (Merrill Lynch)? As we learned in Chapter 6, Egos Gone Wild, you'll have to be nimble and make changes because Berkshire Hathaway municipal bond insurance could deteriorate. Passive bond portfolio management no longer means you can be asleep at the switch.

Additionally, we would like to not worry about these bonds being called. If possible, stick to non-callable bonds with varying

Table 9.1 Bond Ladder

Year	Principal	Coupon income
Year 1	$100,000	$5,000
Year 2	$100,000	$5,000
Year 3	$100,000	$5,000
Year 4	$100,000	$5,000
Year 5	$100,000	$5,000
Year 6	$100,000	$5,000
Year 7	$100,000	$5,000
Year 8	$100,000	$5,000
Year 9	$100,000	$5,000
Year 10	$100,000	$5,000

maturities. The objective is to build a sequence of bonds maturing every year—called a laddering strategy. For example, say our old acquaintance, *El Greedo*, wants to put $1 million of his holdings into a quasi-passive discipline. He targets specific maturities over the next ten years so he can still have some reinvestment upside in the event interest rates fall but won't suffer too much should they rise. Essentially, he's what the techies call *interest rate agnostic.* Over the ten years of his maturity ladder, it will average out for him regardless what rates do. Here's what his maturity ladder looks like (see Table 9.1).

Notice how *El's* principal matures throughout the ten years. He also gets a steady income that is totally safe. No single position (unless it's a prerefunded bond or one that is escrowed to maturity) should represent more than a 5 percent allocation. Also, it is fine to skip a year on the ladder if you can't find an appropriate bond that matures that year.

Very smart for *El* to allocate a completely reliable segment of his portfolio to the passive strategy. However, he's more of hands-on guy. *El* will employ more active strategies too. Let's see what he does.

Indexing Strategy: It's Best to Use a Bond Fund

This strategy lets the professionals create your bond portfolio for you. Think of it as a semi-passive discipline. It takes some of the thinking out of portfolio management. However, you must first find a bond index whose performance you like. Then you must buy a bond fund that tracks that index. Many such indexes hold a lot of bonds. The professional managers rebalance the portfolio periodically for you.

There are all sorts of indexes around. Three of the most popular are:

1. iShares Barclays Aggregate Bond (AGG).
2. iShares iBoxx investment grade corporate bonds (LQD). The iShare iBoxx corresponds to investment-grade corporates as defined by the iBoxx Investment Grade Index.
3. Vanguard Total Bond Market (BND). This ETF also tracks the Barclays Aggregate Bond Index.

The iShare Barclays Aggregate is interesting in that it is the successor to the Lehman Aggregate Bond Index before Lehman Brothers when bankrupt. It still retains its popularity among bond investors. It attempts to mimic the results of the total U.S. investment-grade bond market. All you have to do is buy the ETF stock that tracks the basket of bonds.

Immunizing Strategy

We mention immunizing more for completeness than for practical application by individual investors. Immunizing can get complicated. It involves creating long positions with durations at the long and short end of the U.S. government Treasury yield curve. In theory investors match short positions with duration in the middle of the curve. These positions protect against parallel shifts and slope changes in exchange for exposure to curvature changes of the yield curve. Enough said.

However, a simpler spin-off can be fairly simple and effective. Let's say that you're retiring in ten years and want to pay off the mortgage balance on your house at that time. Ten years from now your mortgage balance will be $300,000. Buy now and hold $300,000 face value zero-coupon municipal bonds that mature in ten years. You've matched the anticipated cash outflow (the mortgage payment) to the cash inflow (from the maturing zeros). This is a favorite technique of corporate treasurers because it immunizes their required cash flows from interest rate risk while matching them with known future cash outflow requirements. Even better, by owning zero coupon municipal bonds there are no taxes due upon maturity.

Active Bond Strategy

This one is for the players. It maximizes total return. Actively managing a bond portfolio requires investors to make bets on a number of moving targets:

- Direction, level, and timing of interest rate moves.
- Changes in the shape of the yield curve.
- Changes in yield spreads across and between various sectors.
- Changes in yield spreads for particular bonds.

There certainly is upside potential if you're right, but significant downside if you guess wrong. Unless you consider yourself qualified to make these decisions and have the time to actively manage this segment of your bond portfolio, there are money managers and bond funds that provide active bond management.

Routine Strategy Evaluation

Every quarter, evaluate your entire portfolio and your strategy. Honestly evaluate reasons you bought each bond. Determine if the reasons you bought each position are still valid. Check out their financial status. Still healthy? What about any bond insurance for your municipal bonds? Has the credit rating of the insurer been downgraded? Is the management team you originally bought still in place and doing the job you expect? Or, has it become decidedly hostile to bondholders by initiating a debt-financed stock buy-back program?

 Action Step: Document Goals; Evaluate Performance

Create your own written checklist of the things that are important to you in evaluating each bond position you own. Also, create written targeted cash flow and yield targets for each segment of your bond portfolio. Then every month go down your checklist for each position and evaluate the performance of each portfolio segment. Where individual bonds fall short of your evaluation criteria and no longer fit your written bond discipline, target them for sale.

This monthly evaluation ensures that you keep your fingers on the pulse of your bond portfolio. It forces you to follow your bond investment discipline. It also organizes your thinking related to the various strategies associated with your bond investments. The more you are informed and actively involved in your own investing decisions, the better. To be uninformed is to be vulnerable. Don't be a victim.

Evaluate Your Team

While you're evaluating your investment portfolio, take a periodic look at your investment team. Your broker should be giving you great ideas for bonds that fit into your strategy and have specific places in your portfolio. Don't be shy. He is paid to help. Let him do his job. If he isn't helping, then replace him with a broker who will do a better job. That's why you always have at least two brokers you work regularly with and maybe a third waiting in the bullpen for his chance to show you what he can do.

If your broker never, ever calls you with a suggestion, then suddenly makes contact, think hidden agenda. He may have a client who needs to dump a problem bond. His inventory may be heavy with a risky bond. He may have learned of an imminent downgrade from his firm's analyst and has been ordered to dump the bonds. If you are an infrequent customer or of no importance to him, be skeptical of such ideas and their source.

For example, we know a very savvy individual investor whose bond salesman called trying to sell him Jefferson County, AL. sewer bonds. His bank's bond department had them in their inventory. The broker explained to the savvy investor how great these bonds were and that they were safe and gave a great yield. The investor didn't really do any research. He just picked up a copy of the *Wall Street Journal* from the day before. There in black and white was an article about Jefferson County on the verge of filing for bankruptcy. Did the broker know about Jefferson County's financial condition? Of course he did. Was he trying to dump a position on an unsuspecting investor? Absolutely.

You've heard about the Chinese wall that supposedly exists between analysts and traders. We already said it has more holes than Swiss cheese. The brokers and bond salesmen may ask analysts to write a few short paragraphs on specific bonds in their corporate inventory or that a major customer needs to sell even when such a report isn't justified. The purpose is to generate something written that can be sent to buyers that rationalize a case for buying the bonds. Yes, this is against SEC rules. Even so, it happens all the time.

Of course, brokers don't look on every customer as an uninformed patsy. But brokers have just one priority every minute they're at their desk: Make as much money for themselves as humanly possible. They are commission-generating machines. With luck and experience you will develop relationships with brokers who follow the rules and aren't too greedy. However, often on the journey to find these rare gems, you will grind through a number of brokers who fall short in living up to the industry's highest ideals.

 Action Step: Firing or Hiring Your Broker

When should you fire a broker? The best reasons are:

- When he offers bonds that are consistently off the market (in basis points and in yield) from where they last traded on TRACE. In essence, he thinks you are stupid.
- He no longer has the ability to offer retail bond issues during the retail order period.
- When you are constantly arguing about price.
- When he can't meet your price.
- When he doesn't acknowledge your counter bid.

These functions are the basis of what you pay your broker for. Terminate the relationship. The act of firing a broker simply requires you to transfer all of your positions to a new broker. This effectively closes the old account. It's important to close that account so you don't have money and bond positions scattered all over town. Consolidate your resources.

Conversely, how do you hire the new broker? As bond market professionals, we advise getting a fixed income specialist (no surprise there). Bonds should be his main business. You do not want a stock jockey who does bonds only when the stock market tanks and there's nothing else to sell that generates commission.

At least one of your brokers should be a major underwriter such as:

- JP Morgan
- Morgan Stanley
- Merrill Lynch
- Wells Fargo

Add a regional such as Robert Baird, Keybanc, RBC Dain Rauscher, or AG Edwards to the mix. Talk to the office manager and ask for the fixed income specialist and hope he doesn't give you the broker of the day (the rotating broker with no further qualifications other than it's his turn to take unsolicited calls).

You don't want a broker who will farm out your account to bond funds or other bond managers. You can do that on your own. Instead, you want a broker who will present valid ideas and reasons that will fit into your specific portfolio.

Research

Bond investing is about research and opinions. Make sure you get updated research reports on your corporate bonds and the sectors in which you have positions. Your broker can help here—usually for free if you are a good customer. Additionally, read, read, read. At a minimum read *Barron's, Forbes,* and *The Wall Street Journal.* Subscribe to a good fixed income newsletter such as our *Forbes Tax Advantaged Investor.* Yes, we're plugging our newsletter here. It's like the political candidate voting for himself. If we didn't think our product was the best, we wouldn't be in the race in the first place.

Get updated S&P and Moody's reports when there's a material event or a ratings change. Study them. Add this information to your evaluation and use it to make your hold or sell decisions.

Avoid the Yes-Men

Everyone learns far more from those who disagree with them. Be sure you have at least one contrarian on your team. This is a voice you listen to who is separate from the pack. He may be a columnist or a TV talking head. Your contrarian balances what the herd says. Often the best investment ideas come from those outliers.

Banking analyst, Meredith Whitney began talking about the banking crisis long before it occurred. She cited all the reasons the U.S.' banking system was about to implode. She was right. She advised whoever would listen to get out of the financials. Listen carefully to those who disagree with you.

Consider What Can Go Wrong

Fixed income investors possess an overarching skepticism. Unlike stockholders, we have limited upside potential. We're in it for the yield and cash flow bonds provide.

So what is a bondholder's worst nightmare? There are so many. Start with a ratings downgrade. This may be a catastrophic event. It lowers the bond's value and could impair the issuer's ability to continue debt service.

Then there is the falling U.S. dollar. This event affects corporate bonds because if the U.S. dollar falls, the foreigners won't buy our Treasuries. This causes corporate bond prices on the whole to fall. Also, issuers that are exporters will enjoy an expansion of their business. That's good for earnings. But as Treasury prices fall and yields rise, their bonds will fall in value. *Sometimes, what's good for the issuer is bad for its bonds.* This isn't so much for the municipal bonds as for corporates, since municipal bonds are purchased only by U.S. citizens.

Since 2008 governmental intervention has become yet a new worry for bondholders. Healthcare is a catastrophe waiting to happen as Congress sinks it fangs into the U.S.' medical delivery system while this book goes to press.

Creditworthiness of a bond issuer and its ability to continue tapping the credit markets is a constant concern to bond investors. We suspect it was a bond *meister* who coined the paraphrase: *A rolling loan gathers no loss.* As long as corporate America continues to roll its bonds and commercial paper, it can probably survive any economic downturn.

These are just a few of the myriad concerns that worry bondholders. There are many, many more. Be on the lookout for bad news associated with your bonds. Equally as important, watch out for good news affecting the bond issuer. It too often works that as stocks go up, bonds go down.

Buy Quality

The spreads between investment-grade bonds and high yield change all the time, just as do the spreads between Treasuries and investment-grade corporates. Staying on top of these moving targets dictates the timing of buying and selling. Individual investors without the considerable amount of time it takes to monitor the bond market and its many indicators have the most success when they stick with good quality. To us, this means holding no bond whose rating is less than BBB (Standard & Poor's and Fitch) or Baa (Moody's). This rating means the issuer has adequate ability to pay interest on time and repay principal at maturity. However, it's not exactly a sterling endorsement. Adverse developments for BBB's are more likely to impair debt service abilities than for a bond rated A and above. BBB– is the lowest of the investment-grade ratings.

An example of a good BBB is the Biogen IDEC, Inc. 6% March 1, 2013 CUSIP 09062XAA1. Biogen is a leader in its field. This bond has a coupon that increases if circumstances conspire to deteriorate its issuer's business and the bonds are downgraded. Additionally, the maturity of this bond in Biogen's debt distribution places it in the middle of some major cash outlays—just where you as a bond investor want to be. The Biogen charts are shown in Figures 9.2 and 9.3.

Seize Opportunities

Just as experienced bond investors create an investment discipline and follow it, so too do they know when to break their own rules. From time to time opportunities present themselves. For individual investors, most come from their loyal brokers. When they learn of breaking news or get some form of intelligence about an issuer (always available in the public domain), they will call their clients. This especially occurs when they already have the bonds in their own inventory.

However, you can be your own information conduit simply by connecting the dots. When you hear breaking news about a bond

GRAB   Corp **DES**

SECURITY DESCRIPTION   Page 1/ 1
BIOGEN IDEC INC   BIIB 6 03/01/13   102.218/102.218   (5.34/5.34) TRMT

ISSUER INFORMATION	IDENTIFIERS	1) Additional Sec Info
Name BIOGEN IDEC INC	CUSIP 09062XAA1	2) ALLQ
Type Medical-Biomedical/Gene	ISIN US09062XAA19	3) TRACE Trade Recap
Market of Issue Global	BB Number EH2397816	4) Corporate Actions
SECURITY INFORMATION	RATINGS	5) Ratings
Country US Currency USD	Moody's Baa3	6) Custom Notes
Collateral Type Sr Unsecured	S&P BBB+	7) Covenant/Default
Calc Typ(1)STREET CONVENTION	Composite BBB	8) Identifiers
Maturity 3/ 1/2013 Series		9) Fees/Restrictions
MAKE WHOLE	ISSUE SIZE	10) Prospectus
Coupon 6 Fixed	Amt Issued/Outstanding	11) Sec. Specific News
S/A 30/360	USD 450,000.00 (M)/	12) Involved Parties
Announcement Dt 2/28/08	USD 450,000.00 (M)	13) Issuer Information
Int. Accrual Dt 3/ 4/08	Min Piece/Increment	14) Pricing Sources
1st Settle Date 3/ 4/08	2,000.00/ 1,000.00	15) Related Securities
1st Coupon Date 9/ 1/08	Par Amount 1,000.00	16) Issuer Web Page
Iss Pr 99.88600	BOOK RUNNER/EXCHANGE	
SPR @ ISS 325.00 vs I 2 ⅞ 01/13	GS,ML	65) Old DES
HAVE PROSPECTUS DTC	TRACE	66) Send as Attachment

SHORT 1ST CPN. CALL @ MAKE WHOLE +50BPS. POISON PUT @ 101% SUBJ TO RATINGS
TRIGGER. CPN STEPS UP BY 25BP FOR EA RAT DOWNGRD BY S&P OR MOODYS FOR EA NOTCH.

Australia 61 2 9777 8600 Brazil 5511 3048 4500 Europe 44 20 7330 7500 Germany 49 69 9204 1210 Hong Kong 852 C377 6000
Japan 81 3 3201 8900   Singapore 65 6212 1000   U.S. 1 212 318 2000   Copyright 2009 Bloomberg Finance L.P.
G407-87-1 11-May-09 15:44:43

Figure 9.2   Biogen IDEC

issuer, think, *how does this affect the bonds this company or municipality issued?* Examples of how information that connects the dots can benefit investors are more common than you might think.

Say that there is a change in the CEO of a corporate bond issuer. Look up his background and what he did at his old company. Was he known for being oriented toward balance sheet improvement—in other words, was he the bondholders' friend? If so, is he replacing a CEO who was not a friend to the bondholders? If this is the case, then you should look for the company's balance sheet to improve. This is good news for bond investors. The bonds may be a good buy now before the new CEO fully takes over and begins working his magic.

Another example has us looking at the ratings. Often analysts speculate in their reports on bond issues whose ratings they think may be upgraded in the near future. A bond upgrade often translates into an uptick in the bond's price. If your portfolio can stand some mild speculation, if you like the bond anyway, *and* if it has a place

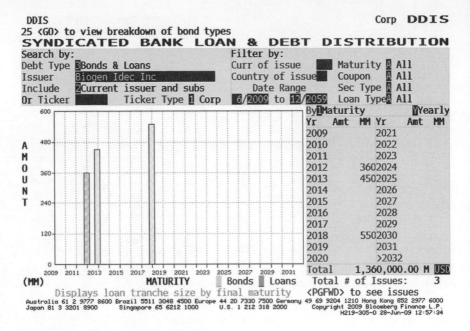

Figure 9.3   Biogen Maturity Distribution

in your investment discipline, then buy the bond on the upgrade rumor.

Love Me Tender

When do you tender your bonds? This is a question every bondholder wrestles with. One the one hand, tendering your bond when asked by the issuer—even with a nicc call premium—stops the juicy yield you may be enjoying. Now you have to replace it in your portfolio. Perhaps you'll be successful in getting the old yield; perhaps not. If you decide not to tender your bonds, you'll get to keep the yield, but may have created a huge problem. What happens if most of the other bondholders tendered? Now the issue is very small and therefore, illiquid. Who are you going to sell the bonds to if you have to get out? You may own these bonds until maturity, biting your nails as you watch the value fall every day.

Action Step: When to Tender Bonds

Smart investors weigh the facts. At the end of the day, though, they will often tender their bonds. Better the devil you know than one you don't. There is no comfort in owning an illiquid, falling bond when you could have sold it and pocketed the call premium. Whatever you decide, be sure to consider your cash flow needs.

Cross-Over Bonds

Some tax-exempts issued by out-of-state jurisdictions may still be exempt from your home state taxation. That's right. They're called multi-state or cross-over bonds. These bonds are not common, but they do exist and can add diversification to your portfolio while maintaining your tax exemption.

Most often cross-over municipal bonds occur when an issuer's reach spans more than one state jurisdiction. Toll bridges serving two states will likely issue bonds exempt from income taxes in both states. The same thing happens with port authorities and airports that support communities in multiple states.

Multi-state tax-exempt bonds are great additions to bond collections for reasons other than just diversification. Most investors in high tax states concentrate their municipal bond portfolios in their home state. That makes sense in order to minimize personal income tax liability. By adding bonds backed by the revenues of multi-state jurisdictions, you spread geographic risk without losing your state tax exemption. You're betting on two state economies rather than just one.

Additionally, it is often difficult to construct single-state portfolios with a sufficient number of non-correlated credits—that is, credits that don't necessarily move in lock-step with the fortunes of that one state. Multi-state bonds provide a chance to lessen your overall portfolio risk.

Finally, multi-state bonds attract a larger investor pool (from two states rather than one). A larger group of investors increases liquidity in case you need to sell the bonds.

The Metropolitan Washington D.C. Airport Authority 4.875% due October 1, 2017 CUSIP 592646EQ2 is a good example. It is pre-refunded so it's backed by U.S. Treasury securities. It is tax exempt in both Virginia and the District of Columbia. The Metro DC Airport Authority serves Dulles and Reagan International airports. Therefore, its bonds draw on revenues from Virginia and the District of Columbia.

Inflation Strategies

So many investors are worried about inflation. No wonder, President Obama's stimulus packages, temporary liquidity facilities, potential national healthcare coverage, and the massive issuance of Treasury debt to pay for it all have terrifying inflationary repercussions.

As a bond investor, how can you protect and manage your bond portfolio in an inflationary environment? There are a couple of solutions. First and most obvious is to load up on Treasury Inflation Protected Securities (TIPS). These bonds adjust monthly to the Consumer Price Index as the U.S.' economy succumbs to the staggering grip of inflation.

The question is when to buy TIPS: before inflation occurs or when it gets cranked up? The nominal yield is low. You're betting that the CPI component will generate a large total return. The answer depends on how worried you are about inflation. Those who think that hyper inflation is just around the corner should buy TIPS now.

On the other hand, since the yield on TIPS is so low and if you don't think inflation will happen for a while, then wait until you get a good whiff of it. Then pounce. Regardless of your opinion on inflation, a great way to get the same effect of owning TIPS is instead to buy the exchange-traded fund for TIPS, symbol TIP. It is liquid just like a stock and has a low management fee.

However, be careful. Many of the TIPS funds including the ETFs omitted their dividends at the end of 2008 and 2009. There's nothing worse than having dead money locked in a vehicle with a no or very low dividend for which you are waiting on inflation to bail you out.

An alternative to the ETF is to buy a Treasury Inflation Protected open-end, no-load TIP fund. Make sure you go with a low cost fund manager such as Vanguard.

We're still on inflation protection. There's a corporate bond for the inflation fearing. They're called CIPS, Corporate Inflation Protected Securities. CIPS have a different structure than TIPS. The CPI component is added to the coupon with a 30-day look-back and is paid out monthly. This gives CIPS holders real cash flow in the event of inflation right now when they need it most, whereas the CPI component of a TIPS bond is added to the principal. So you don't get the inflation protection payment until it matures or you sell it.

There's a risk with CIPS—almost all of the issuers are financial institutions. This means the issuers are the remaining brokers and insurance companies. Therefore, you can't diversify your industry risk with CIPS—you're limited to strictly financials.

Deflation Strategy

It may sound odd, but should the pundits somehow be wrong and instead of inflation the U.S. economy sinks into a deflationary spiral, there's one and only one bond to buy: long-term Treasury bonds. There's no risk of credit quality, and your total return will get the most bounce for the ounce. The equity bear market of 2008/2009 taught us that Treasuries are always the safe haven for capital.

Strategies for a Cratering U.S. Dollar

Watch the value of the U.S. dollar. The direction of the dollar can foretell a lot about the Federal Reserve's stance on interest rates. If the Fed wants to support the dollar, it will raise interest rates. Without raising interest rates, but still trying to support the dollar, it'll resort to the less effective jaw boning and moral suasion. The Fed wants a stronger dollar but won't raise interest rates for fear of upsetting a fragile economy.

 Action Step: Falling U.S. Dollar

What to do if the dollar falls: Hedge the dollar by buying a foreign currency ETF and/or non-dollar denominated bonds in the form of a no-load bond fund or ETF.

A Safe Bond Portfolio

Putting all the theories contained in this chapter into practice, let's see what a safe bond portfolio looks like. Say an investor has $1 million to invest in his bond portfolio. He lives in a state with a low state

Table 9.2   Safe Bond Portfolio

$1 Million Safe Bond Portfolio			
Description	Coupon	Maturity	% of Assets
Corporates:			
AmerisourceBergen Corp Spnt	5.625%	9/15/2012	2.5%
Tyco Electronics	6.000%	10/1/2012	2.5%
Biogen Idee	6.000%	3/1/2013	2.5%
Best Buy Inc NT	6.750%	7/15/2013	2.5%
Verizon	4.750%	10/1/2013	2.5%
Kraft Foods Inc.	5.250%	10/1/2013	2.5%
Altria Group Inc	8.500%	11/10/2013	2.5%
Conagra Foods Inc	5.875%	4/15/2014	2.5%
GATX Corp	8.750%	5/15/2014	2.5%
Microsoft Corp	2.950%	6/1/2014	2.5%
Coming Inc	6.050%	6/15/2015	2.5%
Fisher Scientific	6.125%	7/1/2015	2.5%
Autozone	5.500%	11/15/2015	2.5%
Cisco Systems	5.500%	2/22/2016	2.5%
Jefferies Group	5.500%	3/15/2016	2.5%
Dupont	2.250%	12/15/2016	2.5%
National Rural Utility Corp	5.450%	4/10/2017	2.5%
IBM	5.700%	9/14/2017	2.5%
Johnson & Johnson	5.150%	7/15/2018	2.5%
Wal-Mart Stores	4.125%	2/1/2019	2.5%
Municipals:			
Dallas Tex Wtrwks & Swrsys	5.000%	10/1/2012	2.5%
Greenville Cnty SC Sch Dist	5.500%	12/1/2012	2.5%
Oklahoma Hsg Single Family Rev	4.200%	9/1/2013	2.5%
Seattle Wash Mun Lt & Pwr Rev	5.625%	12/1/2013	2.5%
Indianapolis-Marion Cnty Ind Pub Libr GO	4.100%	7/1/2014	2.5%
Missouri St G.O. Bds	5.250%	10/1/2014	2.5%
Springfield Ill Wtr Rev	5.400%	3/1/2015	2.5%
Arizona St Transn Brdgrant	5.000%	7/1/2015	2.5%
Ohio St Infrast Impt	4.000%	9/1/2015	2.5%
Virginia St Res Auth Infas Rev	5.500%	5/1/2016	2.5%
Illinois St Ref GO	5.500%	8/1/2016	2.5%
Puerto Rico Sales Tax Fing Cor Rev	4.000%	8/1/2016	2.5%
South Dakota Brd Reg	4.125%	4/1/2017	2.5%
Sugarland Tex Wtr Wks & Swr	4.000%	8/15/2017	2.5%
Madison Wis Prom Nts	4.250%	10/1/2017	2.5%

Table 9.2   (Continued)

$1 Million Safe Bond Portfolio			
Description	Coupon	Maturity	% of Assets
Chicago Ill Brd Ed	5.000%	12/1/2017	2.5%
Nacogdoches Tex Indpt Sch Dist GO	4.000%	2/15/2018	2.5%
Pflugerville Tex Indpt Sch Dist GO	4.000%	2/15/2018	2.5%
San Felipe Del Rio Texcons Indpt Sch Disl GO	4.200%	8/15/2018	2.5%
Shelby Cnty Tenn GO Pub Impt Sch	4.750%	3/1/2019	2.5%

income tax rate. He wants 50 percent in corporates and 50 percent in tax exempt municipal bonds. The main concern is capital preservation. Here's what this investor bought to create a safe bond portfolio (see Table 9.2).

The take-away from Chapter 9 is that now bond investors finally have the tools to safely manage their portfolios. Five years ago, we had nothing so effective. Next, we take you deep inside the bond trenches, where few retail customers venture. Chapter 10 shows you the ugly underbelly of the bond market. Don't miss it.

CHAPTER 10

Horror Stories from the Bond Trenches

Bond horror stories both in the midst of the 2008/2009 credit crisis and after could fill a book by themselves. Through the last nine chapters your faithful authors have addressed and shared some of these problems. Nevertheless, they linger on, mounting bigger and bigger losses for unsuspecting bond investors. Institutions and money managers still find it difficult to believe the wide bond spreads—the spreads between Treasuries and other bonds—and the bid/ask spreads. As the spread to the Treasuries widens, bond prices fall. As the spread between the bid and the ask widens, buyers and sellers move farther apart on what each thinks the same bond is worth. Neither spread is good for the individual investor.

Bond Pricing Inconsistencies

Have you tried to sell a bond for which you couldn't get a bid and you were left holding the bag? You're not alone. The big institutions that do this for a living have sometimes experienced the same thing. At the height of the credit meltdown, often those on the trading desks didn't know how to price even the plainest vanilla prerefunded, escrowed municipal bonds.

Here's a perfect example that occurred on June 25, 2009, with San Francisco Airport 5% due May 1, 2032 CUSIP 79765AL95. They were prerefunded May 1, 2012 @ 100 and used 100 percent SLGS as collateral. In other words, these bonds were as safe as any bond ever will be. One would think that the prices for such a plain vanilla bond would be very tight. Instead, we got offerings all over the map from different dealers:

- 30 bonds offered at 1.70% yield to the prerefunded date.
- 440 bonds offered at .77% yield to the prerefunded date.
- 10 bonds offered at 1.75% yield to the prerefunded date.
- 25 bonds offered at 1.519% yield to the prerefunded date.

The difference in price between the lowest yield (highest price) and the highest yield (lowest price) amounted to $22.48 per bond. Not much, you may say. Unless you are an institution that is buying several thousand. The person who bought the 440 bonds at .77% yield over paid by $9,891.20 ($22.48 × 440 bonds = $9,891.20). This overpayment was equivalent to 2 percent on the total purchase of $492,008. So, right out of the blocks he was down 2 percent and would have to make that up just to get even with the price he should have paid.

We've cautioned you to buy the largest bond issues to maintain your liquidity in case you need to get out. Yet Bondland's new landscape sometimes doesn't give a guarantee of liquidity even for the largest issues. Sometimes getting bids on bonds we want to sell is difficult or impossible. Other times, we get an avalanche of bids with price differences so vast you could park a double-wide trailer between them. Sometimes you just never know what will happen when you go to sell your bonds.

Consider the investor who was trying to sell his Pelham, New York, Union bonds 4.000% due August 15, 2020 CUSIP 705795JG. The bids he received didn't tie with what TRACE was reporting, so he called a total of nine brokers. Of these, eight provided bids. They ranged in price from a top of 100.31 to a low of 95.224—a 6 percent difference. That's a lot on a bond.

Why did this happen? The Pelham bonds are triple-A rated. It's a large issue so liquidity is no problem. Further, these are state intercept bonds (though in New York they are called State Aid). So in the event that Pelham can't make the interest and principal payments, the state steps in to make them money good. These are plain vanilla bonds with absolutely no hair on them.

The reasons for such price inconsistency could be many. We'll never know. Perhaps the broker may not have known the bond and reflected the risk of the unknown in his bid. Or, he may not have had a home in which to place them. He reflected this holding risk in his bid. There could be other reasons.

Action Step: Price Fluctuations Between Bid and Ask

Protect yourself from large price fluctuations between brokerage firms. Before bidding or offering a bond, first look up the most recent trades on TRACE (see www.investinginbonds.com for access to the TRACE system). Next, see where the issuer's newly issued bonds are trading. The secondary market should be relatively closely reflected in the new issue prices. Any prices bid or asked that differ substantially from what the brokers are saying means they are off the market. Move on.

Broker's Business Mutations

The bond brokerage industry has mutated itself into several sub-businesses since the 2008 credit meltdown. It's important to know which business you're dealing with—the rules have changed in each.

Agency Versus Principal Trade

The number of bond trading desks has shrunk due to the consolidation of the brokerage industry. Brokerage firms have less capital to invest in bond inventory, and they're no longer willing to take the holding risk. Often, they don't have the bond a customer wants to buy in their inventory. Nor do they want to inventory bonds on which every client needs bids.

They first try other customers. If that customer isn't using the TRACE system and doesn't know the market for the bond, the broker may be able to steal it. But if that doesn't work, the broker has to go out to other brokerages to get bonds. When this happens, he often charges a principal mark-up to his customers. This is a much higher fee for bonds as if this was a risky trade and the broker actually held the bonds in inventory. But it was a risk-less trade and the broker didn't hold the bonds in inventory. He bought them from the other broker who held them in *his* inventory. Okay, so maybe the bonds hit the broker's inventory account for a second or two before going right back out to the retail customer. Even so, such trades should be charged the lower agency fee rather than the much higher principal fee.

 Action Step: Principal Versus Agency Fees

Ask which fee—principal or agency—you were charged for a trade. If the broker didn't hold your bonds in inventory, then yours was an agency transaction. You should be charged the lower agency fee. Complain if the fees you are charged don't make sense.

"I'll Work the Order"

During the 2008/2009 credit crisis this phrase enjoyed resurgence in its dubious popularity. When applied to a sell order, "I'll work the order" means that the broker is unwilling to buy the bonds from the customer without an immediate buyer on the other side of the transaction. He's afraid of getting stuck with unwanted bonds in his inventory that he might have to sell at a loss just to get rid of them.

For a buy order, it means the broker isn't willing to borrow the bonds from another broker (short the bonds) and sell them to the buyer. So tight is the bond market that brokers don't know if they'll be able to cover the short at a profit later. If such things happen to professional, seasoned institutional bond investors dealing in sizable lots, imagine what happens to individual investors. Those of us who manage bond portfolios encounter this every day.

When a broker says that he'll work the order, just know what he's really saying. Contrast that to the broker who can make an immediate commitment and execute your transaction into or out of his inventory right then.

New Issues Are Now a Private Placement

After the 2008 credit crisis there was such a huge market for corporate bonds that most new issues were oversubscribed by all the big institutions. There is no retail order period for corporates as there is for municipal bonds. Individuals cannot hope to get into new issue corporate bonds without some sort of special connection. The only way most individuals can buy corporate bonds is on the secondary market.

Essentially, the new issue corporate bond market became a private placement market. The bond issue manager calls his corporate friends asking how much he should put them down for. The issue is sold to the institutions before the individual investors ever see it.

That's just the way the market has evolved. Individual investors are relegated to the secondary corporate bond market. This makes it that much more important that you be informed about the corporate bond in which you're interested. Know the pricing history. Understand the rating. Make good and sure of its fit in your collection of bonds and just what it will do for you. Before calling your brokers (always more than one) to place a bid, have a firm price range at which you will graciously take it off the broker's hands. Once you have these things in place, then go hunting.

No Bids, Now What?

You own a bond that you no longer want in your portfolio. Problem is, neither does anyone else. You can't get a bid—not even from the broker who sold it to you. This not only happens to retail investors but institutional investors as well. Why? Maybe the issue is illiquid. Could be there's no other market for the bond. Why would a broker buy a bond he can't sell to someone else at a profit? The broker wants to turn his inventory. That's how the coins that once jingled in your pocket now jingle in his.

Getting the impression that the brokerage industry has no conscience? You're right. There is a solution: Tell your broker that when he offers you a bond meeting your criteria and that has a place in your collection you will buy it. Make good on your promise. However, also tell him that this relationship must be a two-way street. When you need a bid, he is obligated to give you a fair price that is on the market and buy back that bond no matter what. After all, you purchased it from him. Individual investors with a few million dollar bond portfolio have this leverage. You're important to the retail brokers. Most would rather have 50 $2 million accounts than a single whale with $100 million in his account. The former is a business. The latter is slavery to a single individual.

What You Don't Know May Hurt You

Individual investors look to the bond market for safety. For decades before the 2008 credit crisis this was how the financial world rolled. It was especially true for the bond funds. Individual bond investors and those who buy bond funds weren't used to losing any money. The worst that usually happened was that the stock market outperformed their bonds and bond funds, so bonds didn't make quite as much money as their neighbors. But they didn't have the risk either.

Then the 2008 credit crisis hit. Losses in bond mutual funds shocked investors. They thought their bond funds provided a barrier from what was happening in the stock market. Not so. The reason was that these investors had stopped watching what their bond fund managers were doing. It was a classic case of what they didn't know that came back to bite them. Here's what happened and how you can stop it from happening to you.

There are a number of bond mutual funds that more or less mimic the Barclays Capital Aggregate Index. This is the most widely used investment grade bond market benchmark index. The Barclays Index did its job—during the meltdown of 2008 it *gained* 5.2 percent. The shock to the bond mutual fund investors was that their holdings *lost*—on average 4 percent. Some of the lowest performers were down 20 percent below the Index. They were supposed to be tracking the Barclays index. So what happened? Why did they lose money when the index they were supposedly tracking made money?

The answer is in what the investors didn't know. They didn't know that their bond fund managers had strayed from exactly tracking the Barclays Index. Yet that was what the investors thought they were paying for. Instead, the fund managers began redesigning the portfolio to take more risk and get a larger return. The media calls it style drift. We call it taking their eye off the ball. They held far fewer of the safest bonds listed in the Barclays index. They exchanged them for more risky bonds (lower rated) that were less liquid.

Like a hurricane in the ocean, when the credit crisis slammed its way ashore, knocking down everything in its path, prices of these risky bonds collapsed. Had these bond funds been doing what they were supposed to and tracked the Barclays Index, they would have had 75 percent of their holdings in AAA rated bonds. Instead, they had just 62 percent by June 2008. Also by then, they had 5 percent of their holdings tied up in junk bonds. What was the Barclays Index percentage of junk bonds? Zero.

The bond managers rationalized their aberrant behavior saying that they weren't being paid to just track an index. Untrue. Their company's clients paid the company to track that index. The company paid the bond managers to execute this tracking discipline. They strayed from their discipline without telling anyone.

 Action Step: Stop Style Drift

Always track your bond fund's portfolio of holdings against what its charter says it will buy. Do this analysis quarterly in line with the SEC's quarterly holdings reporting requirement for mutual funds. If it deviates, then determine if the newly styled fund still fits with your investment discipline. If not, then dump the fund.

Broker Errors

After 30 years in the bond market, we've never seen so many brokers making such large pricing errors. These occur mostly on requests for bids on bonds that we bond managers are seeking to sell. Brokers confirm a bid price. They do the trade and generate an electronic trade ticket. It posts to TRACE. Later, the salesman calls, claiming he made a mistake and the price will be lower than what you thought you sold at. The broker is asking to back out of the trade or ask the customer to accept the lower price (cancel and correct at the lower price).

This could be intentional. It could be that brokerages have downsized staff to the point that the system is more error-prone than before. We don't know the reason, just that the problem exists.

What can you do if this horror happens to you? Tell the broker the trade stands as you agreed and as he committed to you. The brokerage firm has the ability to eat any loss to retain a customer. Your broker may argue with you. He may not have the authority to make good on your trade. Ask to speak with his supervisor or the office manager. If you still don't get satisfaction and if the amount at stake is worth the trouble, you can always file a complaint and take the broker to arbitration. Usually the mere threat of such action does the trick.

In any case, such errors happen. We're dealing with imperfect human beings. If it happens more than once or twice or if you suspect it was something other than an honest error, move your account to a more careful brokerage firm. You must have confidence that when you execute a trade it will be done as agreed. The bond market is a microcosm of life—your word must be your bond.

Government Intervention

This is perhaps the biggest horror story of all. The threat and actions of our federal government intervening in private enterprise has been both a blessing and a curse depending on who is talking. At the height of the federal government's *de facto* nationalization of the major U.S. banks—in March of 2009—bank bond prices dipped to their absolute lowest.

Why? Wasn't this supposed to be a solution rather than throwing more gasoline on to the fire? Bondholders saw what the government did to preferred shareholders of Fannie Mae, Freddie Mac, and Citigroup. By denying payment of preferred dividends to the preferred shareholders of these institutions, the government wiped out billions in investor holdings. The rationale was explained by the need for shared sacrifice. The bureaucrats in Washington appointed themselves as those who would choose who is going to share the sacrifice. They started with preferred shareholders.

Bondholder reasoning went: If the government wiped out the preferreds, what's stopping them from doing the same thing to us? Prices for unsecured, senior, and subordinate bank debt plummeted. A good illustration of this carnage is on the Merrill Lynch Senior Unsecured shown in Figure 10.1 (which now carries the Bank of America name).

Note that the price bottom of this bond occurred in March 2009—the height of the government's talk about shared sacrifice. This Merrill Lynch bond (now called Bank of America) carried a price whose yield to maturity was 11.75%. Junk bonds yield in this range.

Not much longer after that, the government cut a deal with Chrysler's auto workers, placing their interests higher than the

BAC 6.4 08/17 $ ↑ **90.121 +1.024**   Corp **GP**
At 09:37 Vol 325 Op 90.121 Hi 90.121 Lo 90.121 Prev 89.097 TRMT

Figure 10.1 Merrill Sr. Unsecured

Source: Bloomberg Finance L.P. © 2009 Bloomberg Finance L.P. All rights reserved. Used with permission.

company's secured bondholders. This was the time in recent U.S. financial history that the government acted in direct violation of the law and reallocated wealth as they chose in order to accomplish a particular goal—to save an industry. Of course, this action will guarantee the UAW votes Democrat come the 2012 presidential reelection campaign.

 Action Step: Governmental Intervention

Consider potential governmental intervention in every bond you buy or that is currently in your portfolio. Two rules to help protect from *de facto* nationalization are first to never have more than 5 percent of the portfolio taken by a particular issue or sector. Next, stay high up on the capitalization structure—around the senior secured area. This may or may not afford adequate protection, but at least it follows the rule of law . . . we hope.

The Culture at Money Funds

There are varying cultures even at the generally conservative money market funds. Investors put their money into money market funds not necessarily to get a great return. Instead, they are a safe, interest-bearing parking place for money in transit to other, more lucrative investments.

You don't want a money market fund whose culture is to stretch for the last basis point in yield when it's so hard to come by. These are the funds that risk breaking the buck—net asset value falls below the $1.00 of value for every $1.00 invested.

This happened to Reserve Primary Fund during the Lehman Brothers' downfall of 2008. The Reserve Fund held $785 million in unsecured debt issued by Lehman. They wrote this down to zero after Lehman filed for bankruptcy. The value of Reserve Fund's holdings after the Lehman collapse was $.97 for each $1.00 put up by investors. Further, to avoid a run on the fund as people scrambled to get out, they put a seven-day hold on all redemptions.

As you do with your bond funds, be sure to monitor how your money market funds are investing. If it looks dicey or the least bit questionable, then move your assets elsewhere.

Underwriting Problems

Some smaller regional investment banks underwrote special tax bonds and tax allocation bonds. These were unrated bonds wrapped with insurance. They used very aggressive underwriting standards because they thought investors could always rely on the insurance if things went south.

The investor's income stream depended on constant property tax revenues to service the debt. Property taxes dropped as real estate prices fell. Property tax reassessments caused tax revenues to drop even further over a larger pool of property owners.

Because of the drop in state property tax revenues, some municipal bond issuers have dipped into their reserves. Their bondholders are now in jeopardy. Many either will go into default or have already done so.

The moral is that a strong economy can mask underlying problems. They always surface at the first sign of trouble. Over the last two years we've all seen more than our share of trouble.

Here's what to do for municipal bonds dependent on property tax revenues to stay afloat:

1. Make sure the property tax base is in a mature, stable area.
2. Stay away from housing developments that rely on the hope that home buyers will move in and pay property taxes.
3. Stay away from regions where the economics and employment resources are declining. Residents have a difficult time paying their property taxes if they've lost their jobs.
4. Try to find a bond with protection. This can be in the form of a prerefunded bond, escrowed to maturity, double-barreled, or a GARVEE.
5. If there is any doubt about the bond, stay out of it. There are so many opportunities out there that it makes no sense to take a risk when you don't have to.

 Action Step: Bond Default

Just one bond default in your portfolio can negate the few added basis points by taking risk you shouldn't have. It's not worth it to jeopardize the overall profit of the entire portfolio by taking risk.

Let's avoid the unpleasantness of these horror stories in your own bond portfolio. Chapter 11 shows the right way to analyze a bond so you don't have to go there.

11

Bond Analysis—How to Analyze an Issuer's Creditworthiness

Our sole purpose in analyzing a bond is to judge the issuer's ability to make interest and principal payments through the maturity of the bond. Once we've answered that one question, we're done for the moment. However, as time goes on, further analysis is always needed. The financial circumstances of the issuer and economy will change. Additionally, the sector and issuer both may undergo cultural, product, and management changes. All of these affect the bonds.

The good news is that there are a lot of perceptive reports on bonds and their issuers done by professional credit analysts. They have access to analytical resources that few individual investors can match. The pros do a lot of forecasting and feeding of assumptions into their mathematical forecasting models. They project over a long period of time—through the maturity of the bond, sometimes 20 or 30 years. Even so, the truth is the professional credit analysts don't know any more than the rest of us when it comes to forecasting the future.

A Case of Conflict

Study the analyst reports on bonds you either have in your collection or are considering adding. You can generally get perceptive analytical reports from your bond brokers. But recognize that the bond analysts who wrote these reports have a conflict of interest. They know that if they write a bad report and put in a sell recommendation on a corporate bond, their firm will never be the bond underwriter for that company again. Too many bad reports and the analyst will likely be told the firm can no longer afford his services.

Know also that there are very few municipal bonds specialists. That's why Standard & Poor's and Moody's have taken over much of the municipal bond analysis. Recall the problems with both of these firms when rating the bond insurance carriers. The corporate culture there for municipal bond analysis may be a little better, but it is still housed under the same two roofs. Be skeptical about what you read.

There is another independent bond research firm that has significant credibility in the industry. *Gimme Credit* (www.gimmecredit.com) provides corporate bond research reports, intraday comments, and credit scores geared mostly to bond professionals. Its Investment Grade Reports provide analyses and recommendations aimed at relative value, capital, and anticipation of changes in credit quality. *Gimme Credit* also provides reports on cross-over bonds (split rated between investment grade and a notch lower) and high-yield bonds. This is considered by many bond professionals a must-have subscription—on par with *Barron's* or the *Wall Street Journal.* If your bond brokers don't subscribe to *Gimme Credit,* then you might wonder what other corners they have cut in obtaining and using the best intelligence available.

Consider analyst credit reports a guideline whose conclusions are based on nothing more than guesstimates. The bottom line is that no amount of bond analysis will save you from a falling market. Conversely, a rising tide floats all boats, regardless of the analytical quality. Up markets are what makes the lazy investors who won't do the analysis their portfolios require dangerous. As the market rises, their holdings draft upward with everything else. The lazy think it's their astute perception of future value. Wrong. They may be up 10 percent, 20 percent, or more. But when the market tumbles down as it did in 2008 and as it always does through economic cycles, they lose far more than they ever gained.

However, good bond analysis, consistently applied to your portfolio and regularly updated, may save you from this trap. More to the point, consistent bond analysis and updating of your intelligence may save you from owning a bond that is downgraded or worse, that defaults. This is what we do all day, every day: projections, analyses, and doomsday scenarios.

Muni Bond Analysis the Professional Way

There are usually just two types of municipal bonds you'll conduct intensive analysis for: general obligation bonds and revenue bonds. For both of these, begin by examining the bond's Official Statement along with the most recent financial statements. Focus on the bond's underlying credit quality and not on the strength of the bond insurer, if any. We no longer depend on the insurance companies to bail us out.

There are just five factors to examine when analyzing a municipal credit: economy, security, legal provisions, finances, and management. As you read the official statement and financials, ask yourself:

1. Where is the issuer located?
2. How is it affected by the national, state, and local economy?
3. How is the issuer's repayment ability related to population growth, average home prices and sales, unemployment rates, and the area's wealth indicators? Does it move directly or inversely from these?
4. The Official Statement should tell you what revenues are pledged and what the issuer must do to unpledge them.
5. Also, is the revenue pledge subject to annual appropriation or voter approvals? Voters and legislative appropriations committees can be fickle. It could be that one day they decide to turn off the spigot, leaving bondholders out in the unfunded cold.
6. Ask if there are any existing or potential litigation issues that can void or reduce the revenues pledged to pay bonds.
7. Look for positive trends in the issuer's historical and projected financial performance. Focus on revenue increases, operating expense reductions, and increases in free cash flow. Also, see if you can determine the issuer's willingness and ability of a credit to pay its obligations. An increasing aging of accounts payable on its balance sheet is not a good sign.
8. Look for disclosure of future debt and capital improvement plans. This will affect debt coverage and the issuer's ability to pay interest and principal on your bond.
9. Review the background of the management team. Look for a history of prudent fiscal controls and successfully servicing the other debt on the balance sheet.

10. Make sure the reserve fund can take the issuer through an economic storm.

Sound cumbersome? You're right, it is. But it's our job. If you manage your own bond portfolio, then it should be your job, too. We want to see at least stable and preferably positive trends in these common factors before making a decision to either keep a bond we currently own or buy a new one.

General Obligation Bonds

There are some specific things we want to know about our general obligation bonds (GOs). First, find out the limitations of the general obligations. As always, look in the Official Statement. A GO bond may be unlimited as to rate and amount and have full access to property taxes for debt service. This is the best. Or, it may be limited to a dedicated source within the issuer's general fund. Not bad, but not quite as good as unlimited.

General obligation bonds usually don't have debt service reserve funds to tap in case of a cash shortfall. Therefore, see if the issuer has financial flexibility with large, diverse revenue streams and revenue raising capabilities in the event things take a turn for the worse.

We want a finger on the issuer's largest revenue source. It will probably be income taxes, sales taxes, or property taxes. We look for safety and consistency in those revenue streams. So determine if the issuer has:

- Growing populations in or near large metropolitan areas.
- A large and growing tax base.
- A diverse group of taxpayers.
- A history of stable financial performance.
- Multi-year operating surpluses (the bondholders' dream).
- Fund balances equivalent to 10 percent of the issuer's expenditures.
- Strong overall demographics and wealth indicators relative to the state and national averages.

Remember that we bondholders are worriers by nature. This list pretty much proves the theory, don't you think? If the answer to any of these questions is no, then the issuer gets a black mark.

Table 11.1   Analytical Indicators for a General Obligation Bond

Indicator	Description
Population & growth	Population, and annual % change
Full value of taxable property & growth	$ amount, and annual % change
Full value per capital	Full value of taxable property divided population
Top taxpayer concentration	Top taxpayor as a % of total full value
Top 10 taxpayer concentration	Top 10 taxpayers as a % of total full value
Net overall debt	Net total bonded debt plus applicable share of all overlapping jurisdictions
Net overall debt per capita	Net overall debt divided by population
Net overall debt burden	Net overall debt divided by full value of property
Debt service to expenditures	Principal and interest due divided by general fund expenditures
Fund balance to expenditures	Unrestricted & undesignated general fund balance divided by general fund expenditures
Personal income per capita	Personal income divided by population, as % of national and/or state averages
Median family income per capita	Median family income divided by population, as % of national and/or state averages
Unemployment ratio	Unemployment rate vs. national average

Each analytical point by itself shouldn't blackball a bond from your collection. However, too many black marks and you should begin to wonder how safe the bond really is and if it has a place in your portfolio. Table 11.1 summarizes the thirteen key points to look for in a GO bond.

Revenue Bonds

Unlike GO bonds, revenue bonds pledge bond repayment from a limited source of revenues. These might be from an enterprise fund or dedicated revenue stream such as a toll road. The most common revenue bonds are lease, housing, hospital, utility, transportation, education, and corporate-backed municipal bonds payable by corporations such as PG&E and Georgia Pacific.

These revenue sectors have some common credit qualities to look for. As always, use the Official Statement and bond indenture as your bible. Look up the bond's security and sources of payment. The security features common to revenue bonds are:

- **Revenue pledges.** A pledge of gross revenue is better than net revenue since there's nothing taken off the top that we bondholders can't get our hands on for repayment.
- **Fully funded debt service reserve funds.** Think of a pool of money set aside just for us bondholders that is dedicated to making our interest and principal payments. Such reserve funds give great comfort to us worrywarts.
- **Additional bond tests and rate covenants.** We want to hold the issuer's feet to the fire. Bond tests and rate covenants are a good way to accomplish that. These ensure the issuer maintains minimum levels of financial stability that we bondholders agreed to when we bought the bonds.
- **The ability to set rates independently of regulatory bodies or local government boards.** This eliminates any political motivations of the governing board when setting rates.

When analyzing a revenue bond, focus first on the strength of the bond security and legal provisions. Next most important is an increasing historical and projected trend of net revenues and debt service coverage. We would like to see debt service coverage from net revenues to be at least 1.25 times for most rated municipal credits (see Table 11.2).

Effects of Recession

Economic recessions have ill effects on municipal bonds. No sector is immune to declining revenues. Issuers need to reduce their annual spending budgets. Some do, some don't. The entire state of California is one that doesn't. That state has made history in its budget deficits and cash shortfalls. Their bonds and bondholders have suffered.

You will see several recessions in your investing career. When these happen, watch for huge decreases in state aid and reductions in bond issuers' primary tax revenue sources: property, sales, personal income, and corporate tax. These cuts affect the general obligation bonds of counties, cities, and school districts.

Table 11.2   Analytical Indicators for a Revenue Bond

Indicator	Description
Net revenues	Gross revenues minus operating expenses
Debt service coverage	Operating revenue minus operating expenses, add depreciation, divided by annual principal and interest
Operating margin	Operating profit divided by operating revenue
Operating ratio	Operating expenses divided by operating revenues
Debt ratio	Total debt divided by total assets
Days cash on hand	Cash divided by operating expenses net of depreciation, times # of days in year

You can insulate your bond portfolio from the effects of recession by limiting exposure to lease obligation bonds that are subject to annual appropriation and issued for nonessential governmental services. Instead, look for higher quality credits with ample reserves and sufficient debt service coverage to withstand a prolonged downturn if necessary.

 Action Step: Recession-Proof Your Portfolio

In a recession go with essential purpose revenue bonds such as tax-exempt bonds issued for large, stable utility systems—water, sewer, electric—rather than all general obligation bonds.

Example of a Revenue Bond Analysis

Let's put all this theory into practice. We'll take a close look at the M-S-R Public Power Agency. It is a California Subordinate Revenue Bond, Series 1997D. Its CUSIP number is 553751JE9. It carries a Moody's underlying rating of A2.

M-S-R is a joint-action public power agency created in California by three participants: the Modesto Irrigation District (50% issuer), the City of Santa Clara (35% issuer), and the City of Redding (15% issuer). Its purpose is to procure electric generation capacity for the three co-issuers. M-S-R issued bonds to in part fund their purchase of a 28.8 percent interest in the San Juan Unit No. 4 Power Plant. Being revenue bonds, they are payable using net revenues of M-S-R. By the way, these revenues include the right to collect revenues under a long-term power sales agreement.

From the Official Statement and bond indenture we discover that the power sales agreement obligates each participant to make unconditional payments. That's their monthly nut. The issuers must pay on a take-or-pay basis, for the monthly power costs of the project, including debt service on the bonds. Further, the power sales agreement continues in force until the retirement of all bonds.

The security and legal provisions for this bond are minimal, but adequate. That's typical for a joint-action agency with take-or-pay contracts. All project costs are passed directly through to the three participants and paid as an operating expense of their respective utility systems. The bonds also have a subordinate net revenue pledge along with a fully funded debt service reserve fund.

Financial Performance   The M-S-R bonds were issued over 10 years ago. So we must get recent operating and financial information from their latest annual financial statements. Take a look at Table 11.3.

Table 11.3   M-S-R Historical Operating Performance

	12/31/2006	12/31/2007
Revenues	$ 87,825	$122,914
less: Expenses	54,562	82,363
Net Revenues	33,263	40,551
+ Deprec. & Amort	10,313	11,079
Available for debt service	43,576	51,630
Annual debt service	36,361	35,811
Debt service coverage	1.20×	1.44×
Operating ratio	38%	33%
Unrestricted cash	22,935	23,226
Plant assets	155,052	175,766
Total assets	250,520	256,287
Long-term debt	362,029	412,875
Days cash on hand	153	103
Debt ratio	145%	161%

M-S-R Power Agency is financially sound. As of December 31, 2007, net revenues increased 22 percent and debt service coverage was 1.44×. That's a lot for a public power agency. We're beginning to see some strength in this issuer. The rate covenant allows the agency to adjust electric rates in order for net revenues to cover debt service by a minimum of 1.10×. Yet the 2007 rate coverage was 1.44×, substantially above the minimum. That's more good news. The additional coverage provides a cushion should revenues available for debt service decrease in 2008 or beyond.

Hold on a minute. Is there anything in the future that may reduce our precious debt coverage ratio? This could be a large capital improvement plan with significant debt issuance expected. A little research reveals no such plans. Our bond analysis for M-S-R is complete. Nothing popped up to make us cringe. If we have a place in our collection for a public power revenue bond, this one could be it. Alternatively, if we already own it, we should keep it as long as we still have a place for it.

Yes, analyzing municipal bonds can be a comprehensive and mathematically rigorous dissection of the issuer. Of course, there are multiple moving parts to understand. However, if you take each component one at a time like we do, the complexity is manageable. Further, you don't have to do everything we did in the M-S-R example. Do the best that you can with the resources available to you and what your bond brokers can provide. Whatever you do will be a lot better than what most individual bond investors do, which is nothing. Develop you own informed opinion on your bond, then make your decision and execute—buy, sell, hold, or pass. Remember, it's your money therefore the only opinion that really matters here is your own.

Spotting a Downgraded Muni

Take a look at your most recent brokerage statement. See if next to the municipal bond name or CUSIP number there's a faintly typed "ME." The "ME" stands for *material event*. It means that something has occurred and it's probably not good. If you have a bond designated "ME," look on the back of the statement or at the end of your online portfolio. It may well tell you that the bond insurer has been downgraded. Drill down a little deeper, and you may find the ME means the municipality had to dip into its interest reserves to pay you.

The citation from SEC Rule 15c2–12 spells out these eleven specific events municipalities must disclose to investors if they occur:

1. Principal and interest payment delinquencies.
2. Non-payment-related defaults.
3. Unscheduled draws on debt service reserves reflecting financial difficulties.
4. Unscheduled draws on credit enhancements reflecting financial difficulties.
5. Substitution of credit or liquidity providers, or their failure to perform.
6. Adverse tax opinions or events affecting the tax-exempt status of the security.
7. Modifications to rights of security holders.
8. Bond calls.
9. Defeasances.
10. Release, substitution, or sale of property securing repayment of the securities.
11. Rating changes.

SEC regulations require bond issuers to disclose these material events in a timely manner to each nationally recognized municipal securities repository or to the Municipal Securities Rule Making Board. The challenge to us bond investors is that these disclosures are often difficult to find and usually not reported in time to avoid damage.

Stay on top of all material events. They may have a material impact on your net worth. The MSRB, through its web site, www.emma.msrb.org, posts material events. Alternatively, you can contact your investment professional for updates on material events. If he can't or won't provide that information, get another professional.

Notification that a material event has occurred is your signal to find out what happened. You well may have a decision to make about the bond. If it was downgraded, then it may no longer fit the risk component of your investment discipline. It is time to get out.

Categories of Strength

When analyzing a bond there's a quick guideline to determine its strength. These four categories have to do with the type of bond it is and how it will be repaid. Even better that the names and types are already familiar to you from earlier chapters. In descending order from strongest to weakest here are the relative strength determinants:

1. **Prerefunded and escrowed:** The safest bonds are the prerefunded, or escrowed to maturity, bonds: Their creditworthiness is guaranteed by a trustee-controlled escrow account consisting of U.S. Treasury obligations. In the unlikely event of default, the bond escrow account becomes the new source of interest and principal payments without skipping a beat. Stay away from prerefunded bonds escrowed with Fannie Mae, Freddie Mac, or Guaranteed Investment Contracts (GICs).

2. **State general obligation bonds:** The issuer has but to transfer tax revenue into the bond payment account to repay bondholders. Further, GOs are senior to all other claims on the state—they're the first to be repaid in the event of a problem, although sometimes there are exceptions.

3. **County and city general obligation bonds:** These lose some strength because they rely on a smaller tax base than the state GOs. Still, county and city bonds can be safe credits as long as the issuing entity's tax base is broad and diversified.

4. **Revenue bonds:** Most revenue bonds are considered money good as long as they have consistent and certain revenue generation. The bonds whose revenue stream comes from toll roads, power plants, and diversified industrial centers are just three that fall into this category.

5. **Revenue bonds with less certain revenue sources:** Among these bonds are tax allocation or certificate of participation bonds. Good examples are the Housing Finance Agencies whose revenue-generating ability may be diminished by an epidemic of home foreclosures. Another less certain issue would be a Hospital Revenue Bond that has a high percentage of revenues derived from Medicare or Medicaid. The security of such bonds declines when municipalities struggle to control soaring medical costs.

Special Questions for Corporate Bonds

Corporate bonds are a different animal from municipal bonds. Along with most of the things we look for in a municipal bond, we also want to know how we're going to be repaid if the company's fortunes turn downward. After all, this is a debt we're owed. Here are two important questions any broker you use must answer for a corporate bond you may be considering:

1. Where is the bond on the company's capital structure? Is it senior secured? Is it subordinated debt? This tells you where in line you'll be standing to get paid in the event of bankruptcy.
2. Where is this bond on the maturity distribution curve? This is just a fancy way of asking what other debt matures before ours does. Ideally, we don't want to be last in a long line of maturities sucking cash from the corporate coffers, then when our turn finally comes, we find they're out of money.

Awareness of the Capital Structure

Capital structure—how corporate ownership is split between equity and debt holders—matters. It always has and always will. Understand how the corporate bonds you own figure into the issuer's capital structure. Are bondholders contributing 50 percent or more to the company's capitalization? Depending on the factors we're about to show you, this could be good, or it may indicate an overleveraged corporation.

For new corporate bond issues, state in any detail how the proceeds will be used. If the company intends using the proceeds to just buy-back its stock, then you might have a problem. Such usage does nothing to help the company earn even $1 more revenue. Indeed, it dilutes the cash available to service existing bondholders.

Determine how highly leveraged your company is. The economic downturn that began in 2008 should have taught us the value of building enough liquidity to survive the economic slowdowns that are sure to occur. The more leveraged a company is, the less margin of error it has, and the more sensitive it becomes to even a tiny downward blip in its revenue. Soon it becomes addicted to commercial paper—short-term debt—at just the time when interest rates begin soaring.

There is no ideal capital structure. The proper mix between debt and equity is constantly changing. As bondholders we judge how well our corporate bond issuers manage that mix. We make that judgment frequently as events unfold. When you assess a company's capital structure, consider several broad indicators:

- The social trends that influence the company.
- The willingness of the capital markets to cough up more cash as needed.
- Government regulation is the new entrant to the equation. For some preferred stock- and bondholders, the government has become the goliath with the ability to swing a sword, devastating to their financial health. We can't ignore that possibility anymore.
- Evaluate the industry in which the company operates and where it is going.
- Judge the state of the economy. Is it expanding or contracting and how does that affect the value of your bond?
- Look closely at the company itself and its management team.

Look at the Big Picture

Bond investors look through a telescopic lens. They must possess the ability to drill down into the minute detail of a particular bond issuer. At the same time, they need to pull that lens in to look at the big picture. That ability gives you an indication of whole industries and sectors in your bond analysis.

For example, let's take a look at the junk bond sector. These are the issuers rated less than BBB–. With just a little light reading, you could know that there was a ton of junk bond debt maturing in 2009—about $178 billion according to *Forbes*. The banks were reducing the lines of credit extended to corporations, not increasing them. If you were back in 2009, you would ask, *can this junk bond debt be refinanced?* Sure it can, providing the issuers can pay the enormous interest rate attached—17 percent, say the experts. That's a pretty big interest rate. It approaches credit card debt.

What about the issuers that cannot refinance their debt? These companies are choking. They will first try to sell assets to raise the working capital needed to stay in business. Of course, they won't be the only companies out there trying to peddle nonessential assets. Their value will ratchet down as supply of such assets increases.

If they can't sell enough assets and if restructuring debt doesn't work, they face possible bankruptcy. That's not only bad news for their bondholders but it will have a tumble-down effect on other parts of the economy such as increased unemployment.

What does this mean to a bondholder? First, take a close look at any junk bonds in your collection. Find out when the bonds mature. If it's in the near future, then make a judgment as to the probability of refinancing if they can't repay the principal from cash reserves. If they probably won't be able to refinance and they don't have the cash to repay the bondholders, then your decision is made. Sell the bonds right now.

If, on the other hand, the company might be able to refinance, then assess its cash position and compare it with liabilities coming due. Does it have enough cash to stay current on its obligations? Determine how its industry is poised to weather any storms brewing on the horizon. Ask yourself if its bank lines are sufficient to pay interest and principal on the bond debt—your bond debt.

All these questions and educated guesses help you form an opinion on holding or selling a bond. Once you've made your decision, act on it. If you decide to keep the bond a little longer because the coupon rate is so good, then watch it carefully. If you elect to sell, don't wait. But also have a place in mind of what to do with the cash proceeds.

Chapter 12, Mission-Specific Instruments, introduces you to some of the most strategically interesting bonds you've ever seen. They're designed to serve a particular purpose in the bond portfolio.

12

Mission-Specific Instruments

Each sector in our bond collection and within that, each bond, has a particular mission. Different bonds can accomplish specific goals for our portfolio. Like a symphony orchestra, they all have to work together doing their various jobs for the whole to succeed. You're probably already familiar with the mechanics of the mission-specific bonds we'll talk about in this chapter. However, the goal here is to begin thinking about them in a different context. We'll describe the specific missions each can perform in the portfolio. Like a baseball coach choosing his game lineup, he would never put the catcher in the centerfielder's spot. Same thing here. We want the right bonds doing what they do best in the right positions.

Remember *El Greedo*? Once he just bought bonds solely for their yield rather than for any strategic purpose. He had no regard for what they could accomplish for the entire portfolio. This was a real mistake. *Greedo* decimated his portfolio with his lack of strategy. But he learned. Now *El* selects the exact bonds with the characteristics needed to fill the right positions and work in harmony with the other bonds in his collection. Let's get to work in identifying a mission-specific strategy and implementing it with the right bonds for the various jobs.

Define Your Portfolio Missions

Each bond portfolio should accomplish several missions. The most common revolve around these goals:

- Income
- Safety
- Liquidity

Most investors favor one of the missions—income, safety, or liquidity—over the others. Still, creating a bond portfolio that is safe, provides sufficient income for your purposes, and has enough liquidity to meet most foreseeable emergencies is fairly mission-specific. We'll select different types of bonds for each mission we're trying to accomplish. Once we've chosen the type of bond, its range in yield, its maturity, and its rating, we'll begin fine-tuning the mission by choosing particular bonds.

Defining the Driver Assumptions

Bond investors have opinions on the trends affecting their portfolios. Opinions are a good thing. When we select the bonds to fulfill our missions, we tailor them to take advantage of where we think the trends are taking the market. The five major trends affecting bond portfolios include:

1. Yield curve
2. Economy
3. Governmental intervention
4. Inflation
5. Taxation

These are the assumptions that drive the mission of the portfolio. They form the basis by which we select particular bonds. Most important, you must prioritize the order of your needs.

The Yield Curve: Fixed Income's Big Picture

A changing yield curve will definitely affect the value of your bond portfolio. Yield curves come in three main flavors: flat, positively sloping (upward), and negatively sloping (downward). Astute bond investors can make money on any of the three. Really astute bond investors can make big money at the inflection points when the yield curve changes direction.

The strongest bond market rallies come when a negatively sloping yield curve begins to flatten, foretelling the end of an economic boom. This means that short-term interest rates are still higher than long-term rates but are coming down. When this happens, the crowd usually gravitates to money market funds and certificates of deposit. They want to lock in those higher yields as the yield curve flattens. Resist the temptation. When CDs expire and money market funds begin repricing down the flattening yield curve, those investors will quickly lose their once-juicy yields.

If you see a flattening, then a yield curve turning positive, your mission is to maximize the value (prices) of your bonds without sacrificing safety and liquidity. Do this by bringing intermediate and long-term bonds into the portfolio. Your non-savvy friends who are sticking with their short-term money funds and CDs will think you're crazy. That's okay. You have a different agenda—one that accomplishes your specific missions.

When the yield curve flattens and eventually becomes positively sloped again (it always does as the economy weakens), you'll participate in the bond price appreciation. When done right, this maneuvers price appreciation into the portfolio.

State of the Economy

As the state of the nation's economy changes, so must your emphasis on safety and liquidity. An economy coming out of recession will experience more available credit. Low interest rates will be history.

It is unbelievably difficult to identify when and how fast our economy will return to a growth path. The 2008/2009 credit crisis—which became the mother of all economic crises—had several false starts. Remember the green shoots the economists thought they saw? Everyone wanted to believe they were real. Alas, the first green shoots were nothing more than a short-lived tease.

Read, study, and listen. Then form your own conclusions about the economy. Is your company laying off employees in droves? Are people you know and read about spending with abandon? Or are they hunkered down saving every dime, afraid to spend for fear they too will lose their job?

The economists sit in their ivory towers, crunching numbers. They are not always part of the cloth of everyday society. They may not drive through local communities where *Going Out of Business* signs shout from every street corner how bad the economy is. They may not have problems getting increased lines of credit. Economists don't usually provide pens, paper, and supplies to the local schools. Their children often attend well-financed private schools where such essentials are provided for them. And most of all—they get paid whether they are right or wrong on their economic calls. Economists are insulated from reality and the impact their errors create.

Ask yourself: "Why weren't these brilliant gurus on CNBC in 2007 and the first quarter of 2008 warning us of financial Armageddon?" The answer is the economists ignored the signs like everyone else. Economic transition periods can be dicey for investors. Everyone is trying to jump aboard the rocket before it launches. There are often many false starts. So evaluate the state of the economy from your own surroundings. Give it your own perspective. It's as good an analysis as anyone else's.

Governmental Intervention

As you begin lining up the industries and issuers within the industry that belong in your portfolio, think about what the government could do. Think the unthinkable. The unthinkable happened to the automotive industry, the financial industry, and the home loan industry.

While we were writing this book, the government was taking aim at the healthcare industry. Investors weren't sure what the government would do. Many weren't waiting around to find out—us included. Healthcare is fast becoming a sector that frightens many investors.

Inflation and Deflation

The potential for rampant inflation is on the minds of many investors. The U.S. government agreed to lend, spend, and guarantee $12.8 trillion in order to stop the economic slump that began in 2008. According to the economic pundits (if they eventually are right), this is a sure prescription for inflation.

How do we protect our bond portfolio from the risk of inflation? One good way is to hedge that risk with Treasury Inflation Protected Securities (TIPS). By putting in a layer of TIPS, a portion of the portfolio's principal adjusts with the consumer price index. The net of this adjustment is added to the principal and is *paid on maturity* of the TIPS bond. As the consumer price index rises, so does the principal.

If you're worried about inflation, you can also buy treasury ETFs that bet on higher yields and lower bond prices. These have all the trading advantages of ETFs and move inversely to treasury bonds. As inflation ramps up and bond prices decline, the value of the long-term treasury ETFs rises. There are two such ETFs with different maturities:

1. ProShares Ultrashort 7–10 Year Treasury ETF (Symbol: PST)
2. ProShares Ultrashort 20+ Year Treasury ETF (Symbol: TBT)

Like most hedges, think of TIPS and Treasury ETFs as an insurance policy against inflation. That is its job in the portfolio. You don't need to insure completely against inflation. That would concentrate too much capital in a single strategy that may or may not come true. However, it will protect a portion of the portfolio from inflation. That's all you need.

Worried about deflation? Long-term Treasuries are your trump card. You can buy Treasury bonds outright, a no-load, low-cost Treasury bond fund or long-term Treasury ETFs. They all work to greater or lesser extents depending on how much capital you allocate to your deflationary bet. Just remember to always think fees. Buy what will cost you the least in fees.

How much of your portfolio should you insulate? Calculations can help you to a point. Beyond that, it depends on how much risk of inflation you are comfortable with. A comfortable hedge would be 25 percent; much more than that and you will give up cash flow to live on. That's because the nominal yield on TIPS is pretty low. And—you are betting on the come that inflation will rear its ugly head. Your payday doesn't happen until you sell or your TIPS mature.

Investors think they can't lose money with TIPS . . . wrong. You are guaranteed par value. If you buy an individual TIPS that has a lot of CPI built into its principal, and the inflationary bogeyman doesn't materialize, you can lose that build-up if you hold it to maturity. Complicated stuff.

A similar inflation hedge is issued by corporations—corporate inflation-protected securities (CIPS). Like TIPS, these provide a set coupon rate and are adjusted for inflation each month according to the published consumer price index. *Since they pay monthly,* CIPS react much faster to inflationary changes than do TIPS. Essentially, they pay at just the time when you need inflationary protection most, rather than waiting possibly years for the TIPS bond to mature and pay the added inflationary benefit in the form of added principal.

However, there is risk. CIPS take on the risk of the corporate issuer. Nothing but their full faith and creditworthiness secures and guarantees the CIPS payments. TIPS, on the other hand, have no risk since they are issued and backed by the U.S. Treasury.

Taxation

During 2009 the pundits all talked about "The New Normal." What would the new normal be for GDP growth? For spending? For consumption? For interest rates? We haven't a clue but—we do know whatever the new normal, it will include higher—much higher—state and federal taxes glommed onto each and every one of us.

America has ramped up its debt burden to Herculean levels. Someone has to repay that debt. It is the U.S. taxpayers. With the additional programs in place—such as national and statewide healthcare—there seems nowhere for tax rates to go but upward.

There are several missions your bond portfolio should accomplish for you tax-wise. First, it should provide an income stream that is taxed at the absolute lowest rate possible. Next, it should provide sufficient liquid cash to pay anticipated tax bills when they arrive.

Remembering that there's a rate for every risk, tax-advantaged bonds offer a lower yield than corporates. That's why taxable equivalent yield is the key calculation for comparing tax-free bonds with corporates. This allows us to compare apples to apples when deciding to invest in a corporate bond versus a municipal bond.

There's a simple formula used to calculate a taxable-equivalent yield:

$$\text{Taxable Equivalent Yield} = \text{Tax Exempt Interest Rate} \div (1 - \text{tax rate})$$

For example, say we're in a 35 percent tax bracket and we can buy a corporate (taxable) bond yielding 6.50 percent. We can also buy a tax-exempt municipal bond that yields 5.15 percent. Which is better?

$$5.15 \div (1 - .35) = 7.92 \text{ taxable equivalent yield}$$

This means that the corporate bond must yield at least 7.92 percent before it gives us the taxable equivalent yield of the 5.15 percent municipal bond. It doesn't in this example; the municipal bond is the better investment. As long as the muni is comparable in maturity and risk and we can use the tax-exempt income, take the municipal bonds.

Most likely there's a part (perhaps even a large part) of your income-producing bond portfolio whose income you want to be tax exempt. For this part stick to municipal bonds *issued by your state of residence*. This provides interest income exempt from all state and federal income taxes.

Interest Rate Management

Leave figuring out the direction and magnitude of interest rate changes to the professional economists. And they only very rarely get it right. Instead, insulate your portfolio from the aberrations of interest rate changes. The technique is similar to the insurance policy concept previously suggested.

We designate a portion of the portfolio for interest rate management. As before, we figure out how much of the portfolio value we want to insulate from a wrong direction change in interest rates and how much we want to take advantage of a correct directional change. That's how much of the total portfolio we allocate to interest rate management. We wouldn't want to insulate the entire portfolio from interest rate changes. That would be too expensive, and it would limit any upside potential for when rates once again move in our favor.

For example, say it seems fairly obvious to you that interest rates will rise over the long term. After all, the U.S Treasury Department gave away billions through the TARP program. But TARP didn't quite have the intended effect. Instead of competing for depositors' funds by raising deposit rates or by offering promotional CDs and savings accounts, the banks generally used the money to shore up their reserves and left deposit rates low. Those banks that could, repaid the TARP money as soon as possible. Along with TARP and the other stimulus programs, the United States has over $12 trillion worth of debt to repay.

Investors know from past booms and busts that when the government printing presses are working day and night, the ultimate end product is inflation—bad inflation. Inflation is particularly bad for bond investors because our purchasing power erodes. That doesn't mean you should throw up your hands and dive pell-mell into commodities, currencies, and other asset classes that previously nuked your net worth.

We can insulate part of the portfolio from rising interest rates using several strategies. One is to buy Inverse Treasury ETFs. The principal behind such a creation is to hedge against the price direction of bonds. That's where they get the name, *Inverse*. For example, as interest rates rise, bond prices will fall. However, the price of the Inverse Treasury ETFs will rise (inverse direction to the bonds).

Another feature of some of the more popular Inverse Treasury ETFs is that they track inversely at *double* the price movement of the underlying bonds. This means that if your bonds fell by 1 percent, the Inverse Treasury ETF would rise by 2 percent. This feature is important when managing interest rate risk because we don't want to allocate more than necessary to this part of the mission. Like all insurance policies, you hope you don't need it; that it was money down the drain. Nevertheless, if you need it, you'll be glad you have it.

Inverse Treasury ETFs such as those offered by ProShare Advisors can do double duty as not only the inflation hedge we suggested earlier but also as a hedge against moving interest rates.

Another security that counters some of the effects of rising interest rates is the LIBOR floater and floating rate bonds. The yield floats with an index; in this case it's LIBOR. LIBOR floaters are structured so that there's a coupon plus you receive a percentage of the three-month LIBOR. The bond will have a maturity—such as five or 10 years. The floating part of the bond resets quarterly as its index moves. A basis point spread is chosen, usually to put the final yield around where a similarly maturing fixed-rate municipal bond would be, but with credit risk built into it.

Floaters provide the benefit of increasing your yield as interest rates rise. Sure their price will fall, but not nearly as much as that of a fixed-rate bond in the same rising interest rate environment.

Another hedge against rising interest rates is the mutual funds that buy bank debt. Bank debt floats. So as rates rise, so does the yield on the bank debt mutual fund.

Action Step: No Agency Step-Ups

You may be told by others that agency step-up bonds are a hedge against rising interest rates. They are not. Government agency step-ups are usually called before investors have a chance to reap the benefit of the step-up feature they paid for. Chapter 13, Developing a Sixth Sense, describes step-up bonds in depth.

How do you protect against flat interest rates? This isn't so serious an occurrence as rising rates that erode the asset value of your portfolio. Flat rates just take your portfolio value nowhere. All investors get to do is collect their interest payments, which isn't so bad. One caution: Flat rates could be a precursor to an inflection point in the yield curve—either transitioning to rising or falling rates. A flat yield curve is the most perplexing and dangerous yield curve configuration. You just can't tell if the slope will go positive or negative.

One way to manage flat rates is with a LIBOR Range Note. Range notes were probably the invention of some smart treasurer who wanted protection from rising interest rates and Wall Streeters who saw another way to mint money. LIBOR Range Notes pay an above-market rate if LIBOR stays within a specific range. The range is specified on a schedule that is part of the note indenture. If LIBOR moves outside of that range, the note payment resets to a lower interest rate or no interest at all.

LIBOR Range Notes produce an above market yield while interest rates remain flat and within the specified range. That's a good thing for investors while it lasts. However, rates have a nasty habit of moving. If you buy range notes while rates are flat, just watch them closely. When you see rates starting to move outside your range, you'll probably just have to grin and bear it. They aren't very liquid.

All-Important Safety Allocation

Throughout this book we've talked a lot about safe bonds. We'll reintroduce them. But as part of a mission specific strategy, every portfolio should allocate some percentage to a very safe component as well as a risk component. The risk part takes advantage of market opportunities. We saw that in the Jefferies & Co. example earlier.

There the bonds had not yet caught up with the stock increase. Even though the Jefferies bonds may have been outside the normal investment discipline, the risk component of the portfolio was able to take them. The investor remained true to his stated discipline but was able to participate in the opportunity the Jefferies bonds presented.

The safety allocation, on the other hand, has more strict guidelines. Say that an investor is 50 years old. He may allocate just 50 percent of his total bond portfolio to the Safe category. This doesn't mean he speculates with the other 50 percent. It simply means there are specific types of bonds he buys (and only these types) within the Safe category.

This strategy assures retirement on his terms. Of course, you knew that. Didn't you? But have you followed it? If you're like most investors, the answer is no. Let's change that right now.

The Safe bond category has a simple mission: Regardless of what happens in the economy, in politics, whatever interest rates do, no matter how bad housing prices get, the interest and principal will be paid by these bonds on time, every time. They are safe. This is money you can rely on without a doubt and with no worry. In Bondspeak we say these are "money good bonds."

How Much to Allocate?

As you age, the allocation to safety rises since there's less time and ability to make up losses. By retirement, the income produced in the safe component of your portfolio should cover all your living expenses. So your life becomes totally worry free. Wouldn't that be nice?

Whatever the allocation to your Safe bond portfolio component, it should be significant. Let's start with no less than 40 percent of the total bond portfolio regardless of your age and go up from there as time goes on. Speculate to your heart's content with your stock portfolio. That's not our responsibility. But err on the side of caution in the safe allocation of the bond portfolio.

Determine how much income you want from the Safe portfolio now and in the future. Then use that number to back into the allocation to the Safe portfolio you will need. Once you know how much money you will allocate to the Safe portfolio, you're ready to begin placing the types of bonds within the allocation.

Safe Components

Begin with cash. Allocate a certain amount to money market funds. They are liquid right now and safe. You know they are not going anywhere unless you say so. And you're not saying so just now.

Next, allocate a good percentage of the Safe portfolio to prere-funded municipal bonds and bonds that are escrowed to maturity. Neither can be touched by the issuer no matter how tough times might become. Typically, the preres will be of short to medium du-ration. The bonds you buy today probably won't help 20 or 30 years from now. That's okay. You can roll maturing bond proceeds into them as the years go by.

Do not concentrate your Safe bond purchases in a single munic-ipality or corporate name. If you don't need state tax exemption in your municipal bond portfolio, then buy them from issuers around the country. If you are staying within your state of residence to get the state tax exemption, then spread your allocation around the state in its various municipalities, school districts, and water districts. As always, buy large, liquid issues. Buy into corporate issues of at least $250 million in size; for munis, since the issues are usually smaller, buy the biggest you can find.

Next, allocate a portion of the Safe portfolio to double-barreled municipal bonds. You'll recall that these are municipal bonds with two independent sources of repayment. Generally, they include rev-enue from the project they are funding and, should that fail, the general obligation fund of the issuer.

Cash Flow Planning

We all have cash demands. The big ones we can plan for. The Safe component of the bond portfolio is a good place to do it. Let's say you have committed $25,000 a year toward your 15-year-old grandchild's college tuition. That payout should begin in about four years.

Here's what to do: Buy $100,000 of zero coupon municipal bonds. The first $25,000 tranch matures in five years; the second $25,000 tranch matures in six years; the third $25,000 tranch matures in seven years; the fourth $25,000 tranch matures in eight years. Because they are zeros issued in your state of residence, they are tax exempt at the state and federal levels.

There is no scrambling around to fund the tuition bills. The money is there, ready to be redeemed and disbursed when needed.

You can apply this bond portfolio cash management technique to any large future cash disbursement.

Outsized Yields

As you finesse the bond market, you'll encounter opportunities. You'll be tempted to take on more risk for a greater return. At first most of these will reveal themselves as traps for the uninitiated and greedy—nothing that an aspirin and a short nap can't take care of until the urge to buy passes. However, with practice and experience, you will see the difference between what is real and what is simply bond broker puffery.

 Action Step: Real Opportunity Versus Puffery

Apply these reality tests to each "great" opportunity you see:

1. Rate versus risk: Is the promised rate greater than the going market rate for a similar risk investment? If the return is greater than the return for a similar risk investment, then there is a problem. Pass on it. No exceptions.
2. Do you understand the bond and its issuer? Does it make intuitive sense? If not, then pass.
3. Does it pass the cocktail party test? The cocktail party test says that if you have the uncontrollable urge to brag about your "great yields" at a cocktail party, then you've taken too much risk. Pass on the bonds.
4. If the broker says he's putting his own mother in these bonds, then hang up the phone. He is not putting his mother in the bonds. Chances are the person making such a transparent claim never even had a mother.
5. Are you beginning to think that you're smarter than the market and this one bond trade is going to prove it? Stop it. You are not smarter than the market. No one is smarter than the market. The market can't wait to punish you for entertaining such blasphemy in its presence. Remember that somewhere, somehow there is always a securities market trading. The market will hear of your arrogance. And the market will beat you for your insolence just to teach you a lesson.

Risk Allocation

You have done an excellent job in creating a balanced bond portfolio. You have separate allocations for income, safety, and liquidity. You have specific bond positions whose mission it is to deal with changes in the yield curve, with inflation and with taxation. Where you have future disbursement obligations, you have zero coupon bonds earmarked for that purpose maturing at the time you will need the money. Every month you review each position in each of the three sectors to be sure they continue executing the missions for which you bought them. You keep up on the financial news affecting your bond positions. You have become a bond *investor.* Bravo.

If you have done all these things, then you have a fine bond portfolio that is fulfilling its mission. There's no reason why you shouldn't allocate a portion of the portfolio to a higher level of risk whose mission is to generate above average yields. The amount allocated should not affect your overall financial plan if it is completely lost. It just may be.

Instruments such as emerging market bond funds or the corresponding ETFs are a good place to take some measured risk. These funds characteristically emphasize high current income and capital appreciation. They often invest at least 80 percent of their net assets in debt instruments of issuers tied economically to emerging-market countries. Some take significant positions in lower quality debt instruments and can execute short sales. Sound risky? They are. You wouldn't want to put a huge chunk of your portfolio into such bond funds. However, their annual return over the last five years is impressive—over 9 percent net of all sales loads.

If an emerging market bond fund is too risky, then take a look at the ETFs. These have all the favorable attributes of a stock—you can get in and out any time during regular trading hours and the price is publicly posted. Being an ETF, the risk is sliced and diced in a variety of ways.

The bond ETFs tend to track the Deutsch Bank Emerging Market U.S. Dollar Liquid Balanced Index (DBIQ). This index tracks returns of liquid emerging market U.S. dollar–denominated government bonds issued by emerging market countries. As of this writing, the DBIQ covered 19 countries including Argentina, Bulgaria, Brazil, Colombia, El Salvador, Indonesia, Korea, Mexico, Panama, Peru, the Philippines, Qatar, Russia, South Africa, Turkey, Ukraine, Uruguay,

Venezuela, and Vietnam. Still, if you want the potential of producing a higher yield in the emerging country bond space, the ETFs should be on your list of considerations.

High-yield bond funds or ETFs are an avenue that is different from the emerging country debt market. The high yield bond funds try to provide a high level of current income. They invest in high-yield, high-risk, below investment grade fixed income securities—junk bonds. They invest at least 80 percent of their net assets (plus any borrowings if they're allowed to leverage) in bonds rated lower than BBB by S&P or Fitch or Baa by Moody's.

With either of these categories, the allocation takes on significantly more risk. But the potential yield is higher as well. They diversify country risk as well as the risk of undue concentration in any one bond issuer. If you are going to take some risk, this is how you do it.

Experienced bond investors develop a sixth sense about what can go wrong in a particular bond issue. Chapter 13 shows you how to hone your own sixth sense to keep your portfolio out of trouble.

13

Developing a Sixth Sense

BET ON THE UNEXPECTED, AND ANTICIPATE ITS COMING

Remember the 1999 movie *The Sixth Sense*, written and directed by M. Night Shyamalan? In the movie a child psychologist is confronted by young boy claiming to see dead people—his sixth sense. Experienced bond investors develop a sixth sense, too. This chapter shows you what to look for in potentially troubled bonds and how to spot opportunities before they hit the press and it's too late. This ability can be learned. All you have to do is believe in your own sixth sense.

Bond Sales Tricks

There are lies, damn lies, and then there are bond lies. Failing to spot a bond lie can be expensive. Some bond salesmen are the masters. The unschooled never even know they've had their pockets picked.

Separating the Fluff: PIK Bonds

Would you lend money a second time to someone who admits he doesn't have the funds to repay your first loan to him? "Oh no," says the bond salesman, "don't be so narrow minded. They're money good. Just a minor cash shortfall is all. And will ya look at that coupon!" What's he talking about?

He's talking about PIK bonds—pay in kind. A PIK bond is debt issued with the option to pay more debt equal to the interest that was skipped if the issuer cannot pay or the bond was issued as an original PIK security. With PIK bonds the bond issuer rather than the bondholder (naturally) has the option of issuing more bonds to cover the interest and principal payment. It is a cash management device used by corporate treasurers who need to horde their cash reserves.

PIK bonds have been around for a long time but became popular again in the buy-out frenzy of 2006. In the wake of the credit crisis they lost favor. However, they are making a comeback in some of the private equity firms with cash flow troubles that cannot turn to the debt markets.

Here's the problem with PIK bonds: If a company is so strapped for cash that it can't make its bond interest payment, then why would we want to extend even more credit instead of demanding payment for what they owe now in cold, hard cash? Yet, if we're a PIK bond-holder we have no choice. We'll receive paper in lieu of an interest payment if the company elects to exercise the PIK option and pay with more bonds.

Eventually, even the PIK bonds—the old ones and the newly issued ones—will have to be paid. The company is digging itself an even greater hole by issuing more debt to pay interest they couldn't pay in the first place. It's no wonder that PIK bonds are coming to the forefront as their issuers opt for payment in kind rather than in cash.

Imagine a fixed income pensioner opening the mail, expecting to see his normal fat interest check from the bond issuer. Instead, he gets a notification that is nothing more than a promise (not even an obligation) to pay in the future in some form—perhaps with more paper. Incidentally, the newly issued bonds are also PIK bonds with the same payment-in-kind option. You can't buy groceries with a PIK bond.

Now that you understand what the bond salesmen are talking about, does it take any sort of supernatural insight to avoid being duped into buying a PIK bond? Let's hope not.

 Action Step: PIK Bonds

Avoid buying pay-in-kind bonds. Every one has a certain amount of hair on it. Investors are more likely than not to suffer a haircut when they go to sell them or if they default.

Stepping Up Can Be a Misstep

Your bond market sixth sense at this early stage in its development may alert you to anything unusual. A higher than market rate is unusual. Listen to your sixth sense warning of greater risk.

The same warning should come when you see a step-up bond. These bonds carry an incentive to compensate investors for "unforeseen" risk while they're holding the bonds. The fact is the only people not foreseeing the risk are those living in a cave.

Corporate step-up bonds usually increase the coupon rate 25 basis points for each rating downgrade. The coupon increases attempt to compensate investors for the added risk they're taking as a result of the rating downgrade. The bond issuer is trying to match coupon with risk. Should there be a rating upgrade, the bond coupon rate falls back down.

Here's the problem with step-up bonds: The net interest costs to the corporation that issued the bonds rise with each rating downgrade. This worsens an already deteriorating cash position. It may well cause yet another rating downgrade, triggering another coupon step-up and an even more serious cash crunch. See how the downward spiral gets worse with each step-up? Step-up bonds are only a theoretical safety net for investors. They may spell the possible beginning of the end for a corporate issuer.

There are also government agency step-up bonds out there. Try your sixth sense on these. Let's say a government agency issued a 10-year bond. Its coupons step up every few years: Say 4 percent for four years, then 5 percent for three years, then another step up to 6 percent after another three years.

But wait. Your sixth sense notices that these bonds are *callable* before each coupon step up. Hmmmmm. Your sixth sense asks what the likelihood is of a government agency step-up being called before the first coupon step-up. Answer: *highly probable*. Most investors never get to see the higher coupon step-up they expected when they bought the bonds. In fact, the step-up feature is just a lure to suck in yield-hungry individual investors.

Step-up bonds may sound like they provide added compensation for added risk. They don't. A default on a $1 million bond portfolio that follows our rule of maximum exposure of 5 percent for any one issue and assuming a 6 percent income would all but wipe out that year's entire portfolio income.

Zombie Bonds

You may have heard of zombie banks. These are banks whose net worth is less than zero—they are the walking dead. Yet they continue to operate using government credit support. Once the government withdraws its support, the zombie banks join the ranks of the truly dead.

Zombie bonds have a similar shaky status. These are seasoned bonds issued by companies that are for all intents and purposes already dead. An example from 2009 is GMAC. Without its governmental subsidy, GMAC would be dead. You might have categorized any GMAC bonds you held as zombie bonds. You were betting that the entity survives and can pay interest and principal. Two other examples are CIT and MBIA.

Categorizing a corporate issuer as dead in all but name is up to the bond investor. At the end of the day, the bond investor's judgment is the only one that counts since it's his money that's at stake.

Why would anyone intentionally buy a zombie bond? What often happens is a broker/dealer gets wind of trouble in a company whose bonds it has in inventory. The broker decides to get rid of them while he can. The broker puts the word out to his sales force to dump the bonds. The salesmen begin calling their clients, touting the bonds and selling them to unwary customers.

Or, you may have a zombie bond in your portfolio. It's probably one you've been lugging around, watching it deteriorate due to a bloated balance sheet and fading credit metrics. It doesn't start out that way. Due to an unexplainable inability to sell, the zombie bond's slow deterioration froze the decision-making process. Remember, holding on to a zombie bond is a decision—usually a bad one.

As always, do not buy any bond without first doing your homework. Determine if it fits into your investment discipline. Stop right there if it doesn't. Still sitting on the fence? Take a look at the company's press releases and financial statements. Do you get the scent of trouble yet? Look up its SEC filings and stock trades done by insiders. If the executives are selling their stock, then why would you want their debt? Look at TRACE to see where the bond is trading and if demand appears to be falling.

Unearthing zombie bonds require more research, work, and judgment than the gift of any real sixth sense. The only perception required is at the beginning when something just doesn't feel right about the bond. That feeling launches the investigation.

Truth or Dare

The brokerage industry is entitled to make a fair mark-up on the bonds it sells. The new issue market is a good example. Underwriters make their money based on the underwriting spread. This is simply the difference between the price they pay for an issue and what they sell it to investors for. Say a bond underwriter manager prices the bonds at 99.5 and sells them for 100.0. Their spread is 0.5. On a $100 million bond issue that 1/2 point spread is worth $500,000. That is fair. It is a fee that is publicly known. That is what you will pay for the bonds if you are lucky enough to get in on a new issue. This is the same price that big institutions pay for the millions of bonds they buy in the issue.

The disparity can come once the new issue is sold out and the bonds are free to trade in the secondary market. Then the broker can sell them for whatever the market will bear. Always look for a hidden agenda when speaking with your bond brokers. The litmus test is and always will be the prices shown on TRACE. If your broker is offering a bond at something other than what TRACE is showing, there's a reason. If it's over the market price, he may well be part of an underwriting group. If it's less than market, then he may have some negative information on the bond and its inherent risk. Either way, it is up you, the investor, to find out.

If you buy bonds online, then you've done all the research yourself. The last part of the research equation is price. Use the TRACE rules we've laid out for you. Remember, chances are the bonds you are buying online are not in your brokerage firm's inventory. Bond offerings are being fed from multiple platforms. Often positions are simply clients offering bonds through their brokers. The subliminal echo you should always hear is, "bid back, bid back, bid back," meaning make a counter bid at a price more favorable to you. Between all the steps from each of the institutions involved to you bidding, everyone is taking a piece out of the bond's yield—your potential yield. That's why you should always bid back even when doing online bond trading to try to recapture some of it. As bond professionals, getting the best price is part of our fiduciary responsibility.

You should bid back too—it's part of your financial responsibility to yourself.

Action Step: Use Multiple Information Sources

When relying on information from a bond salesman or online, always use collaborative resources. Never act on the word of a single broker. If you have two opinions that differ from one another, then get a third.

Fitting the Bond into Your Portfolio

Your sixth sense should be attuned to your bond discipline. Know when a bond being offered to you doesn't really fit into your portfolio. Brokers can be excellent salesmen trying to justify a place for their bond in your portfolio. If it sounds like someone is trying to fit a square peg into a round hole, then step back.

Review your investment discipline. Go over again what you want a particular bond to do. Ask the broker to explain just how the attributes of his bond match your requirements. If the explanation doesn't hold water, is too complicated, or has elements that you still don't understand, then simply pass on the bond.

We usually request a couple of minutes of explanation. If a broker can't explain a deal in a few minutes or less, then either he doesn't understand it himself or it's too complicated. Do not just blindly trust the bond salesman's opinion that a bond will do what you want it to. Insist that a prospective bond really does fit into your portfolio before you buy it. Stick to your investment discipline. Don't deviate just because the broker wants you to buy the bond. After the deal settles, he's on to another customer but you have to live with the transaction perhaps for years.

Here's a Great Deal!

There are occasionally some great deals in Bondland. However, it usually takes a market professional who works full time in the industry and who trades in size with a number of brokers to find them. Great deals rarely drop from the sky into the laps of individual investors. It could happen. But then, so too could the Mets win the World Series.

If the rate being offered is off the market, find the reason. Assume it is not that the bond was mispriced and that you are getting the great benefit of someone else's error. As always, there's a rate for every risk. On those occasions when the market is wrong, the pros pounce on it and gnaw at the advantage until it is gone. This doesn't take long.

Recall the Jefferies bonds we described in Chapter 8. In the example we found a great deal for individual investors. But, we created the deal by doing our homework. We looked up Jefferies stock. We reviewed the TRACE history of the bonds. We formed an opinion that the institutional bond investors had overlooked Jefferies. So we acted ahead of them and were rewarded with a whopping yield. We also shared this coup as a recommendation in our *Forbes Tax Advantaged Investor* newsletter.

Reading the Market

Tune your sixth sense to what signals the market is giving you. For example, say that share prices run up but bond prices stay the same (rather than drop as you would expect). You know something is happening. Someone is right and someone is wrong here. The stockholders might be incorrectly running up the stock price, covering their short positions. The bondholders are standing pat because they know better. Or the bondholders have made a mistake in not selling, thereby allowing the price to fall. Either way, there's an opportunity for someone.

If you pay attention to the markets, you will develop that sixth sense for opportunities. Just connect the dots as we described here. Do your research. Create a logical reason for taking action. Then execute. You won't always be right. But with practice, you'll be right more often than wrong.

If you don't trust your sixth sense, then hire a professional money manager. That's what we professionals do every day. The best ones who have been in business for 20 years or more have a well-honed sixth sense for spotting opportunities as well as trouble.

What the Talking Heads Are Really Saying

The financial press—both print and broadcast—has its agenda. It is to sell advertising for their network. If they should somehow impart useful, accurate, and actionable information along the way, then it is purely an accident. You've probably developed a sixth sense for the financial press by now. Listen to it. But apply the skills you've learned from your bond investing to act as a filter.

Beware the Touts

Touts are the guests appearing on the financial television networks throughout the trading day. They are generally mutual fund managers and money managers. Sometimes they'll drag corporate CEOs in front of the cameras.

Touts are not paid for their appearances. So why do they take their time to go on television? They are there solely to promote their own agenda. The mutual fund managers are there to get viewers interested in buying their mutual funds. The money managers want to show how smart they are so viewers will give them more money to manage, thus boosting their income. Equity managers generally sound bullish so that viewers will hire them. The corporate CEOs are there to tell the story their boards want the public to hear—whether true or not.

We bond investors listen to these interviews with our sixth sense at full attention. We understand why these people are on television. We wonder what can go wrong if the point being made is incorrect. We ask how we can survive if things go south. We bond investors are defensive. It usually takes a lot for us to become bullish on the market. But when we do, we jump in with both feet. Our sixth sense is a highly developed filter of all news that is financial.

An example is General Electric back in 2007–2008. The touts were bullishly flogging the stock over the airwaves. We bond investors listened. We looked at the bond spreads to see the more pessimistic viewpoint. We discovered the spreads were much wider than such a high valued industrial bond should be. This signaled a huge down side risk in GE. The touts were still telling viewers to buy the stock. In fact, the only thing holding up GE's earnings was GE Capital—its financing arm. That was about to take a dive. As the financial companies suffered the credit meltdown, so did GE Capital.

What About the News Media?

The news media has 24 hours of time to fill with content. Most of their news sources are the touts with their own agendas. This doesn't make their stories useless. It just requires the filter of reason and your sixth sense.

Get actionable news from the news media. It isn't always easy to find. Due to the necessity for having something on 24 hours a day, much of what we hear isn't really newsworthy at all. Often the reporter is trying to create a story where none really exists just to fill a time slot.

Listen for leading questions and multiple choice answers being furnished by the reporters to the experts. Chances are the reporter has formed an opinion she wants the world to hear. She's trying to put her words and personal opinion into the mouth of someone credible and get them to say it for her.

Reporters compete for air time. They have to sell their story first to the editor or producer. This isn't always easy to do. They have to make their story sound earthshaking to get it green lighted. Often we find the stories that sounded good when pitched lacked any real substance once they hit the air. Nevertheless, the network had a time slot to fill so they went with it anyway.

Find Actionable News

Actionable news contains information that, if true, you can use to make a decision. Actionable news rarely comes all at once. Usually, it's a trail of breadcrumbs that leads you to a conclusion on which you can act. If you do see a news item that you decide to act on, beware that it is quite possibly the unsubstantiated opinion of someone whose agenda you aren't certain of.

The General Motors bankruptcy of 2009 is an example. Many people continued holding their GM bonds when bankruptcy was inevitable. This was the most completely documented bankruptcy of all time. All you had to do was follow the trail of breadcrumbs:

1. The federal government gained control over GM by loaning it money.
2. The federal government then fired CEO, Rick Wagner.
3. The federal government created a Car Czar to oversee its automotive holdings.

By then the company was history. Investors with even a scintilla of sixth sense were out of GM bonds before it declared bankruptcy.

Another example of following the breadcrumbs to actionable news is the 2008 merger of Merrill Lynch and Bank of America. You may recall when then–Treasury Secretary Henry Paulson summoned the Wall Street CEOs to the Treasury Department. The topic was whether to rescue Lehman Brothers. This was a huge news item by itself. Things didn't work out for Lehman.

However, for BOA bondholders, the biggest news item to come out of this meeting was the announcement of the merger between Merrill and BOA. As the months ticked by, the mortgage market kept falling. The CDO market was imploding. All financials—not just Merrill and BOA—were cratering. Spreads on bank bonds were dramatically widening.

Still the Merrill–BOA merger plowed ahead. Astute bondholders wondered why. What did BOA see in Merrill that the rest of the world didn't? All these news items weren't just bread crumbs, they were breadbaskets. They led bondholders to the inevitable conclusion that something was wrong with this merger. BOA was heading down the wrong path. The final decision was to get out of both bonds. It turned out to be a good decision in the short run because the bonds went much lower.

Looking Over Your Shoulder

Bond investors with a sixth sense for trouble are constantly looking over their shoulder. An area to keep on your radar is healthcare. It is high on the government's agenda. President Obama has convened healthcare summits. After all, healthcare is a real vote generator. The next Presidential election in 2012 is not that far away.

Any intervention by the government in America's healthcare system will have adverse effects on the publicly traded HMOs like Cardinal Health and WellPoint. The drug companies like Pfizer and Johnson & Johnson will be adversely affected. Instrumentation manufacturers like St. Jude Medical and Boston Scientific will be brought to the federal government's heel.

What should you tune your sixth sense for? First, watch for regulatory constraints on healthcare executive compensation. There may be pricing restrictions and profit limitations. Dividends to shareholders may be chopped. None of this is good for bondholders. As your sixth sense follows this trail of breadcrumbs, you may come to one actionable conclusion: Get out of healthcare.

Our final chapter cements the principals of post-credit crisis bond investing with Lessons Learned. Mark Chapter 14 with a sticky note and keep it handy throughout your trading day. A quick glance should cure you of any temptation you might have of doing something you shouldn't.

CHAPTER

14

Lessons Learned

We bond investors learned a hard lesson during the credit crisis of 2008/2009. That's when all fixed income sectors except Treasuries let us down. The lesson is that when the unthinkable happens, diversification of your bond portfolio doesn't always save the day. However, the broader lesson is that, just because the bond market swooned, it doesn't mean your credits were bad. In deed, the good ones came roaring back. All the credit research and trading discipline you exercised in creating your bond portfolio worked, assuming you didn't panic and jump off the cliff like lemmings.

We learned a lot about ourselves and our investment discipline during the market crisis. Such introspection forces us to examine what part of our investment strategy failed and what kind of investors we really are. This last chapter points out some of the lessons every bond investor eventually learns. For most, these are expensive lessons. For others—like you—learning from others' mistakes is a far better (and cheaper) alternative.

Investor Not Speculator

Remember *El Greedo*? He used to be a speculator. He bought his financial company bonds because he thought they were *in play*—that he could get a quick pop up in price and then get out. He didn't do any kind of analysis on the bonds; he just bought the name and a hunch. He chose bonds the same way some chose their wine—if they like the label, they buy. When *El Greedo* did see price appreciation in his bonds it was for reasons other than improvement in its underlying fundamentals.

Speculation isn't all bad. Indeed, Chapter 12 described how to invest in outsized yielding bonds. However, speculators must be willing to accept the real possibility of losing some, or all, of their principal. Additionally, using a speculator's strategy, you will not create a lifetime of sustainable income.

On the other hand, *investors* analyze bonds. They craft their investment discipline and strategy to give them exactly the results they designed their portfolio to produce. They have a well-substantiated reason for buying every bond in their collection. Investors make their decisions based on facts. They keep on assessing each position regularly to be sure it still does its job. When it doesn't, they kick it to the curb and sell.

El finally got religion. He turned himself into an investor. He took control over his brokerage relationships. He no longer let brokers talk him into buying a bond for no other reason than it gave the broker his daily commission.

When he did call to place an order, there was no question as to what mission he wanted the bond position to accomplish in his portfolio and why. He also knew the market price for his bond targets.

At first this change may have frightened his brokers. After all, here was a customer on whom they could count for a certain amount of commission just by appealing to his greed. Now there's this, this, *investor* on the line. He's telling *them* to go into the market and get him something specific or as close to it as possible. And always at a tough price. Worse still, *El* had the disturbing ability to walk away from a trade if he didn't like it. Imagine.

Eventually, the brokers came around. The astute investor that *El* turned himself into was more than just a customer. He was the best kind of valued client. He was current on the market news. He tested his brokers by pushing back on what they said. He made them think. He forced them to earn their commission. He insisted they raise their level of service up to his high standards. Together, client and broker became a profitable investment team. The affiliation and longevity of such solid, successful relationships are far more enduring than the *Greedo* of old.

Be Resourceful

There's no question that it is difficult to find new bond ideas. Chances are they won't come from your bond brokers. Most seem to always recommend the same things: Financials, industrials, utilities. A good way to get out of this rut is to review Morningstar's list of bond mutual fund holdings. See what positions the bond funds have. Be sure to look at the laggards as well as the top-ranked funds. It's equally as important to know what *not* to buy as to what you should buy. Look at the municipal bond funds as well as the corporates. Once you have some new ideas, see which ones might fit your strategy, your investment discipline, and a hole in your bond collection.

 Action Step: Watch the News and Act

Business changes at an accelerating speed. When news that affects your bond portfolio hits, you must act. You must act quickly. You must act decisively. Whether it is news that causes you to buy a bond or sell one out of the portfolio, just do it.

Timing is an issue for many investors. The most successful ones get their news, make their decisions, and execute on them at the very beginning of the business day. For those on the west coast, this means getting up early to cull through the news so you have your decisions made and are ready to execute when the bond markets begin trading at 5:30 A.M. Pacific Time.

Don't Bet on the Outcome

As we write this final chapter, the sub-prime corporate lender, CIT, is in the news. It sits on the edge of bankruptcy without a government bailout. CIT had lost money for eight straight quarters. It accounted for lending to just 1 percent of the total U.S. retail and manufacturing. There are many of CIT's competitors that can pick up the slack. This was not a case of being too big to fail.

The point with CIT and other such companies begging for a bailout is not whether it will survive and repay its bondholders. It doesn't matter to our investment strategy what happens to such companies. At the first hint of trouble, astute investors are out.

Investors don't bet on the come. Guessing and speculating are not our business. You can always go back in and rebuy a position you sold for all the right reasons. If things work themselves out and the company survives, the bonds may be stronger and a little pricier from where you sold them. Consider the premium you must now pay over your old selling price as a type of insurance payment. The "insurance premium" is a fraction of the huge haircut on the bonds you would have surely taken had the company gone under and was forced to liquidate its assets.

Close Friends; Closer Enemies

Many people think the famous line, "Keep your friends close and your enemies closer," came from the movie *The Godfather.* Actually, the ancient Chinese military general, Sun-tzu, came up with this nugget in his 400 B.C. masterpiece, *On the Art of War.* The thought is true of bond investors today, except that we have no friends. Only enemies. Each is trying to clip you for a point here, two points there. It all adds up. Be professionally skeptical of everything you read, see, and hear. Consider what ulterior motives your information source may have for dripping this intel on your head.

Among the bond investor's long list of enemies is the federal government. Not for its tax rates. We control that with the municipal bond allocation of our portfolio. Our enemy within the government is its trillion-dollar bailout and stimulus plan. We aren't saying this is a good or bad thing for the nation as a whole. We're only speaking here about our bond investments. With these plans, the government has embarked on a venture it knows nothing about, is ill-equipped to manage, and can only end badly for bond investors.

Do not assume that government decisions related to the financial markets are based on sound economic principles or are even legal as we have loudly suggested. Government decisions are based on political expediency. Make this fact work for you instead of against you.

Keep close to the news on what the federal and state governments are doing that affect your bond holdings. As you see them about to take action, get out of the bonds that could be affected. Remember that you can always buy them back if things should work out.

A working example is the Stimulus Program results. So far, after spending just $102 billion (13 percent) of the $787 billion stimulus package, this much seems clear:

- Banks were hoarding their cash, trying to survive instead of lending in any appreciable amount.
- Those who wanted to borrow could not because the lending standards were out of their reach.
- Those who could borrow didn't because they felt they needed to save for retirement, not mortgage it.

This created a drastically reduced multiplier effect. The Obama administration had counted on a substantial multiplier effect for its Stimulus Package to kick-start the U.S. economy. No multiplier effect meant only a weak, little pop from a Stimulus Package packing $787 billion of explosive power that has so far fizzled.

Another group on the bond investor's list of enemies is the Wall Street banks and the brokers who work for them. Both are motivated by unprincipled, personal greed. They will say and do anything that furthers their goal of putting as much money in their pockets as fast as possible. The good news is that you're in control with your yes or no vote on their recommendations.

The large money managers are not far behind. They are motivated by generating fees. Fees turn into coins jingling in their pockets. These are the pundits who court the financial media. Such people actually have very little to do with their company studying, selecting, or trading securities on your behalf. They are the asset gatherers whose job it is to convince those with the money to give it to someone else in their company to manage.

If you want to see the money managers who will actually make the decisions related to your bond portfolio, look for those who are less visible. They're busy making investment decisions and don't have the time to give away for free to television. These are the people whose competence you need to judge before hiring a money management firm, not their asset gatherers.

 Action Step: Pulling Money out of a Money Manager

It is bad news having to beg to get your money out of a brokerage or money manager. At best it is an overt tactic to keep what's left of your money so the money manager can continue to get fees on it. At worst, it foretells a Ponzi scheme, in which case you'll never see your money again.

Many investors are finding money manager performance does not justify the fees charged. Even better, the investors are doing something about it. A study by Boston Consulting Group found that global assets under management fell 18 percent in 2008. This came after a steady 12 percent increase for each of the preceding five years. The same thing happened in the United States as total assets under management fell to $22 trillion in 2008 from $28 trillion in 2007.

 Action Step: Money Management Fees

Watch the fees charged by your money manager. Compare his fees with those charged by index funds. Did your manager do well enough to justify his fee over the lesser fee charged by the index funds? If not, then replace him.

Pick Your Entry and Exit Points

Always have an entry and exit point for every bond position. This is not always a price. It may be a preset confluence of events that takes place. Establish a decision point that compels you to buy or sell. Write it down. Compare it against progress toward or away from your decision point every day. When the time comes, execute.

Entry Examples

With a little practice, it's easy to establish your entry points. For example, let's say that you've been watching the bonds of a pharmaceutical company. You've studied its product line and its R&D pipeline of new products. You know its debt coverage ratio is slimmer than you would like. However, you've been following its new drug protocol as it makes its way through the FDA's review process. If approved, it appears that this drug could create another new and dependable revenue stream—one that could raise debt coverage up and over your buy threshold. Your decision point to buy the bonds could be when the company announces FDA approval of its new drug.

Another entry point example could be when a management team decides to hold cash rather than pay out the customary annual dividend to stockholders. This is a decidedly bond-friendly move. You've been watching the financial press for the major bondholders calling for this dividend cut. You decide that if and when it happens, you're a buyer of the bonds.

Exit Examples

Where to begin? There are so many. Say that you've been watching the management of a company whose bonds you own. They have been talking up a stock purchase program whose purpose is to raise the price of the company's stock to where it properly reflects where management thinks its real value should be. Of course, the management team has a boatload of options that are currently out of the money, and the clock is ticking on their expiration. The balance sheet tells you that they don't have sufficient cash to execute the stock buy-back. Where will the money come from to fund the stock purchase? You have decided to get out of the bonds if they announce that the stock buy-back funds will come from debt—a very bond-unfriendly move.

Another exit point is the announcement of government intervention of any kind. We've beaten the healthcare dilemma into the ground with good reason. Whether it works or doesn't is not our decision point. The jeopardy into which it places our healthcare corporate bonds if it doesn't work is not worth the risk to us. Our decision point is the announcement of a governmental healthcare program that will impact our healthcare corporate bonds and municipal hospital bonds. We get out at that point. We wait to see the shakeout in the market. If the government's healthcare plan works, we can always jump back into the bonds.

The interest coverage ratio is another exit point quite easily employed since it is quantitative. Establish an interest coverage ratio that appears safe enough for the company to continue paying its debt obligations until it comes to your bonds on the maturity timeline. Maybe for corporates it's 3 or 7 or something in between. As soon as it falls below your safe point, sell the bonds.

Let's go back to management. Bond investors value consistency and anything that is a known quantity with a track record of being bond friendly. If key members of a bond-friendly management team leave, there's a real risk that they will be replaced by those less disposed to keeping the bondholders happy. Certainly the

Board Chair, the CEO, and the CFO fall into the category of key management.

Many are fired simply because the stock price has languished. We hold bonds, not stock, so that's not our concern. The successors have the job of raising the stock price in the very near term. The things they must do to accomplish that are usually not in the bondholders' best interests. Your decision point is to sell your corporate bonds once the bond-friendly managers are fired.

Here's an exit point along the same lines, but not so immediate. Say the CEO of your corporate bond issuer wasn't particularly bond friendly. The board fires him. Good riddance you may say. But what can you do with that information? His successor's reputation isn't particularly bond friendly or unfriendly. You just can't tell. So you decide to give the new CEO a limited time to accomplish his job. You specify what your triggers will be—perhaps interest coverage again. If, after your time limit has expired, he hasn't performed, then get out.

Plan for the Downside

Most of us are optimists by nature—except when we become bond investors. Then we begin looking for the dark clouds on the horizon. It stands to reason. Stockholders buy the stock because they want it to go up. They look for good news. Bondholders own bonds for their interest and principal payments. The day bond investors buy is as good as it gets, and it could go down hill from there. Bond investors look for the downside in everything that could affect their holdings.

The biggest lesson that municipal bond holders learned from the credit meltdown of 2008 was that it can get so much worse than you ever thought. To counter that, municipal bond investors learned to keep a substantial part of their portfolios in safe instruments:

- General obligation bonds.
- Prerefunded and bonds escrowed to maturity.
- Essential service bonds.
- Revenue bonds that carry double-barreled payment protection.
- Revenue bonds that aren't appropriated every year by the state budget.

Action Step: Avoid Swaps

Never buy a municipal bond without first reading the Official Statement. Among the things you're checking for is any indication that the issuer entered into interest rate swap contracts. If so, then you're no longer interested.

Two lessons learned from our Keep It Simple files include:

1. If you don't understand the explanation, then don't buy the bond.
2. If the yield is above the market rate for similar bonds, something is wrong. Pass on the bond.

Your friends may say that the explanation just wasn't presented in a manner that you could understand. Or, that they understand it, why can't you? Fine. Maybe they're smarter or have a more erudite broker to explain it to them. Not your problem. A big part of any successful bond investor's discipline is that he insists on understanding the bond. If he doesn't, then the story ends right there. No wracking your brain, trying to get your head around a convoluted story. Indeed, the more complicated a bond, the more that can go wrong. The lesson here is: *We don't do complicated. We do simple, clean, clear.*

Then there's the over-market yield on a supposedly similar risk bond. The lesson here was, is, and always will be: There's a rate for every risk. If you are offered a bond whose yield is more than that of a supposedly similar risk bond, then conduct a simple test.

Find another bond with that yield and check its risk attributes: rating, type of bond, any guarantees, and insurance—all the things that affect risk. Then assume the bond in question carries that risk. Ask, does that risk fit my bond discipline and does it have a place in my portfolio? If it does, then consider it. What you've done is correctly matched the yield to the right level of risk, then made your decision based on actual facts.

Identify Pockets of Risk

They're not that difficult to find. The difficulty is in believing what you've found and taking appropriate action. Among the biggest problems in the 2008 financial meltdown were interest rate swaps and collateralized debt securities. That's behind us. Is there another equally large or even larger problem out there? You bet. Wall Street's greed knows no bounds. The question is how to find the next big problem so you can avoid it.

Find out where Wall Street is making its outsized revenues. Study it. Try to understand it. It will be a type of security. Maybe it's a new one. Perhaps it's a new wrinkle on an old one. Ask, does the security in question have any real purpose? Or was it created just as a vehicle to make commissions and profits?

This is where it becomes cloudy. Some abused securities, such as credit default swaps, started life with a real purpose. CDSs had the legitimate intent of laying off risk to another party in the event the original creditor defaulted on its loan. The problem came when Wall Street discovered that a market existed for these things that had nothing to do with its original purpose. They began creating CDSs as trading rather than hedging instruments.

 Action Step: Securities with No Purpose

Steer clear of markets materially affected by securities with no apparent legitimate purpose. Don't stop there. Make sure that the corporations and municipalities you own have also steered clear in their dealings. Unwary treasurers and city finance administrators are the prey of Wall Streeters looking for their next big score.

It's Never Over

You may recall the government's agreement in 2008 to guarantee 90 percent of Merrill Lynch's losses if Bank of America would just buy the company. The government was desperate to find a home for Merrill. Agreements were drafted. The public thought the deal was done. Press releases crackled over the airwaves with breaking news to that effect. Six months after the fact BOA said the agreements were never signed and they were still haggling over the $4 billion fee they agreed to pay the government for its guarantee.

The lesson learned is that it's not over 'til it's over and sometimes not even then. Deals struck between big finance and big government always have big money on the line and even bigger egos. Don't take a bond position that depends on one side of the deal performing something specific. Recent history teaches that not everyone always acts in good faith. We don't want you to be caught between them and come out the loser.

Factor In the Variables

When looking at a bond to bring into your portfolio or one that you may need to sell, learn the lesson of considering all the variables. Look beyond the obvious events that drive the issuer's revenue. Try to figure out what else may happen either good or bad to the revenue stream.

An example is the embattled finance company, CIT, in 2009. During mid-2009 it was clearly struggling. Some investors who held CIT bonds hesitated selling them. They thought that the government might bail out CIT. The government was a huge variable in this case. It was in the position of releasing some bailout funds to CIT so that it might live or withholding the life-giving infusion, thus sentencing it to a painful death. At this writing, we don't know what happened. However, prudent bond investors don't care. They saw the risk and were out of the CIT bonds before this game of financial chicken really got started. If CIT survives, investors can always jump back into the bonds.

 Action Step: The Government Variable

Don't make a decision based on a particular direction or decision any governmental body makes. The decision may go your way; it may not. The government may make no decision at all. Or it may go in an entirely unexpected direction. Government has recent history of doing all four. The federal and state governments are now unpredictable. Therefore, they represent a risk to bondholders. Stay out of their way.

Closing

The bond market is huge—much larger than the stock market. It moves depending on so many variables over which investors have no control. Yet, fixed income investing done the right way as described in this short book can provide the financial safety and security you and your family need.

We hope you have learned the lessons of *Bonds Now!* We also hope you have enjoyed reading it as much as we did writing it. Our last parting Action Steps in case we failed to make the point clearly are:

 Action Step: Closing Words

First, always, always, always, use at least two brokers in all of your bond transactions. Any fewer is financial suicide.

Second: Failing to consult the TRACE system for current bond prices before executing a transaction is like driving while blindfolded. Don't try it.

Third: Stay focused on your specific mission while listening to your Sixth Bond Sense will keep your money working for you at maximum velocity.

Finally: We wish you happy, successful, and profitable investing.

Best wishes,
Marilyn Cohen & Chris Malburg

Index